Date Due

JE 07 07			
MAY 0 9 2014			

BRODART, CO.   Cat. No. 23-233-003   Printed in U.S.A.

Winston Churchill

These and other titles are included in The Importance Of
biography series:

Alexander the Great	Harry Houdini
Muhammad Ali	Thomas Jefferson
Louis Armstrong	Chief Joseph
Clara Barton	Malcolm X
Napoleon Bonaparte	Margaret Mead
Rachel Carson	Michelangelo
Charlie Chaplin	Wolfgang Amadeus Mozart
Winston Churchill	Sir Isaac Newton
Cleopatra	Richard M. Nixon
Christopher Columbus	Georgia O'Keeffe
Marie Curie	Louis Pasteur
Amelia Earhart	Pablo Picasso
Thomas Edison	Jackie Robinson
Albert Einstein	Anwar Sadat
Dian Fossey	Margaret Sanger
Benjamin Franklin	John Steinbeck
Galileo Galilei	Jim Thorpe
Martha Graham	Mark Twain
Stephen Hawking	H.G. Wells
Jim Henson	

THE IMPORTANCE OF

Winston Churchill

by
William W. Lace

Lucent Books, P.O. Box 289011, San Diego, CA 92198-9011

Library of Congress Cataloging-in-Publication Data

Lace W. William
    The importance of Winston Churchill / by William W. Lace
       p. cm.   (The Importance of)
    Includes bibliographical references and index.
    ISBN 1-56006-067-0
    1. Churchill, Winston, Sir, 1874-1965—Juvenile literature.
2. Great Britain—Politics and government—20th century—
Juvenile literature. 3. Prime ministers—Great Britain—
Biography—Juvenile literature. 4. World War, 1939-1945—
Great Britain—Juvenile literature. [1. Churchill, Winston, Sir,
1874-1965. 2. Prime ministers. 3. World War, 1939-1945—
Great Britain.] I. Title. II. Series.
DA566.9.C5L28   1995
941.084'092—dc20   94-38561
[B]   CIP
                                       AC

Copyright 1995 by Lucent Books, Inc., P.O. Box 289011,
San Diego, California, 92198-9011

Printed in the U.S.A.

Contents

Foreword

THE IMPORTANCE OF biography series deals with individuals who have made a unique contribution to history. The editors of the series have deliberately chosen to cast a wide net and include people from all fields of endeavor. Individuals from politics, music, art, literature, philosophy, science, sports, and religion are all represented. In addition, the editors did not restrict the series to individuals whose accomplishments have helped change the course of history. Of necessity, this criterion would have eliminated many whose contribution was great, though limited. Charles Darwin, for example, was responsible for radically altering the scientific view of the natural history of the world. His achievements continue to impact the study of science today. Others, such as Chief Joseph of the Nez Percé, played a pivotal role in the history of their own people. While Joseph's influence does not extend much beyond the Nez Percé, his nonviolent resistance to white expansion and his continuing role in protecting his tribe and his homeland remain an inspiration to all.

These biographies are more than factual chronicles. Each volume attempts to emphasize an individual's contributions both in his or her own time and for posterity. For example, the voyages of Christopher Columbus opened the way to European colonization of the New World. Unquestionably, his encounter with the New World brought monumental changes to both Europe and the Americas in his day. Today, however, the broader impact of Columbus's voyages is being critically scrutinized. *Christopher Columbus,* as well as every biography in The Importance Of series, includes and evaluates the most recent scholarship available on each subject.

Each author includes a wide variety of primary and secondary source quotations to document and substantiate his or her work. All quotes are footnoted to show readers exactly how and where biographers derive their information, as well as to provide stepping stones to further research. These quotations enliven the text by giving readers eyewitness views of the life and times of each individual covered in The Importance Of series.

Finally, each volume is enhanced by photographs, bibliographies, chronologies, and comprehensive indexes. For both the casual reader and the student engaged in research, The Importance Of biographies will be a fascinating adventure into the lives of people who have helped shape humanity's past and present, and who will continue to shape its future.

Important Dates in the Life of Winston Churchill

Winston Spencer Churchill is born at Blenheim Palace. — **1874**

1882 — Attends St. James School near Ascot.

Attends Thompson sisters' school in Brighton. — **1884**

1886 — Father, Randolph Churchill, becomes chancellor of the exchequer; resigns same year.

Enters Harrow School at the bottom of the lowest class. — **1888**

1893-94 — Enters Royal Military Academy at Sandhurst; graduates eighth in his class.

Death of Randolph Churchill; Winston joins Her Majesty's Fourth Hussars; visits Cuba. — **1895**

1896-97 — On duty in India, sees action with Malakand Field Force.

First book, *The Story of the Malakand Field Force*, is published; accompanies Kitchener to the Sudan. — **1898**

1899 — Resigns from army; makes first political speech; is defeated in first run for Parliament; goes to South Africa as war correspondent, is captured, and escapes.

Returns to England; is elected Conservative member of Parliament for Oldham. — **1900**

1904 — Switches to Liberal Party; is elected at Northwest Manchester.

Is appointed to first office as undersecretary of state for the colonies. — **1905**

1908 — Becomes president of the Board of Trade; is defeated at Northwest Manchester, elected at Dundee; begins to work with David Lloyd George on social reform; marries Clementine Hozier.

Becomes home secretary; sends police to put down labor unrest in Tonypandy. — **1910**

1911 — Becomes First Lord of the Admiralty.

Start of World War I. — **1914**

1915 — Resigns from the Admiralty after failure of the Dardanelles campaign; joins army in France.

Rejoins cabinet as minister of munitions. — **1917**

1918 — World War I ends; Churchill becomes Minister of War and Air.

Becomes colonial secretary; travels to Middle East to make political settlement; negotiates Free State Treaty with Irish leaders. — **1921**

1922 — Is defeated at Dundee in general election.

First volume in *The World Crisis*, Churchill's history of World War I, is published.	1923	
	1924	Is elected at Epping in general election; rejoins Conservative Party; becomes chancellor of the exchequer.
Resigns from Conservative Party leadership over India policy; enters political "wilderness."	1931	
	1933	Begins warning against German rearmament.
Begins warning about growing German air strength.	1934	
	1936	Supports King Edward VIII during abdication crisis.
Munich agreement gives half of Czechoslovakia to Nazi Germany.	1938	
	1939	Germany invades Poland to begin World War II; Churchill is made First Lord of the Admiralty once more.
Germany overruns Belgium, Holland, and France; Churchill becomes prime minister; makes "blood, sweat, and tears" speech; Battle of Britain is fought in the skies.	1940	
	1941	Meets for first time with U.S. president Franklin D. Roosevelt; Atlantic Charter is signed; Japan attacks Pearl Harbor; United States enters war.
First meeting with Soviet leader Joseph Stalin; major British victory at Battle of El Alamein in North Africa.	1942	
	1943	Meets with Roosevelt in Casablanca, Washington, Quebec, and Cairo; attends Teheran conference with Roosevelt and Stalin.
Combined British, American, and French forces invade Normandy; Churchill intervenes to save Greece from communism.	1944	
	1945	Yalta conference with Roosevelt and Stalin; Germany surrenders; Conservatives lose in general election and Churchill resigns as prime minister; Japan surrenders, ending World War II.
Gives "Iron Curtain" speech in Fulton, Missouri.	1946	
Conservatives win in general election; Churchill once more becomes prime minister.	1948 1951	*The Gathering Storm*, first volume in Churchill's history of World War II, is published.
Receives the Order of the Garter (becomes a knight).	1953 1954	Suffers serious stroke that keeps him out of Parliament for four months; is awarded Nobel Prize in literature.
Churchill College is established at Cambridge University.	1955 1958	Resigns as prime minister.
Dies at London home; is buried at Bladon near Blenheim.	1963 1965	Is made an honorary citizen of the United States by act of Congress.

Man of Destiny

We all leave footprints on the sands of time. Most are very small. Some are large. Only a few, however, are so huge as to turn the tide of history. These giant footprints most often are observed when, at a crucial time, exactly the right person steps forth. If ever a man met his moment, he was Winston Churchill in 1940.

One after another, the nations of Europe had fallen before the armies of Nazi Germany and its leader, Adolf Hitler. Only Great Britain remained, and it, too, seemed certain to be conquered. Certain members of the cabinet, some of the highest officials of the British government, talked of surrender. Churchill, the government's leader as prime minister, refused to listen. "If this long island history of ours is to end at last," he told the cabinet, "let it end only when each one of us lies choking in his own blood upon the ground."[1] His colleagues stood and cheered.

Churchill's fighting spirit rallied his fellow Britons and enabled them to hang on until the war, now known as World War II, was won. The history of the twentieth century turned on the years 1940 to 1945, and Churchill dominated those years. Writer George Bernard Shaw said, "The moment we got a good fright, and had to find a man who could and would do something, we were on our knees to Winston Churchill."[2] A member of Churchill's staff

Winston Churchill was perfectly suited to face the challenges of World War II. During the war years, Churchill's oratorical skills and fighting spirit rallied Great Britain into continuing the fight against Hitler.

wrote, "It was by his strength of will—it might almost be said that it was by his strength of will alone—that we were carried through the greatest crisis in 1940; and this quality continued to inspire his leadership throughout the war."[3]

Churchill's public career spanned more than sixty years. He had enormous influence as a social reformer, as a writer and historian, and as a military innovator. His chief importance, however, is that he saved Britain and, in so doing, may have saved the rest of the world, including the United States.

The Hand of Fate

Churchill thought it more than luck that he was on hand when his country most needed him. He had remained untouched when friends on all sides were killed under fire in Cuba, India, South Africa, and France, and he believed there was a special reason. "This cannot be accident; it must be design," he told his doctor, Lord Moran, at the height of the war. "I was kept for this job."[4]

If Churchill believed it was his destiny to save Britain, he also believed it was Britain's destiny to save the world from Hitler. This hero of the twentieth century was, in his own view of the world, very much a product of the nineteenth. Born in 1874, he grew to manhood during the last twenty-five years of the reign of Queen Victoria, when Great Britain was all-powerful and more than a fourth of the world's population were subjects of the British Empire.

He was, wrote biographer William Manchester, "the last of England's great Victorian statesmen, with views formed when the British lion's roar could silence the world."[5] The British of the nineteenth century simply could not imagine their country losing a war. Winston Churchill in the twentieth century felt the same. He believed that no matter how enormous the odds against it, Britain would win in the end. Britain finally did win, mostly because Churchill would not allow her to lose.

Winston Churchill was not a modern politician. He said what he thought, not what he thought the people wanted to hear. This old-fashioned approach was exactly what Britain needed in 1940. Lord Moran wrote, "Everywhere men were yearning for a man who would tell them the truth, however unpalatable; they were sick of politicians. In Churchill they surely found the man they were seeking."[6]

The grins on the faces of Hitler (right center) and Mussolini (far right) belie the savage ruthlessness the two leaders showed in trying to conquer Europe and the world during World War II.

1 The Naughtiest Boy in the World

Winston Spencer Churchill was never one to wait his turn, even in being born. He appeared two months ahead of schedule, at Blenheim Palace, ancestral home of the dukes of Marlborough. Labor pains overtook his mother so suddenly that she could not reach her bedroom and was taken to a small room off the main hall.

It was there, on the morning of November 30, 1874, that Winston arrived. No baby clothes or cradle had yet been bought, so these had to be borrowed from women in the nearby village of Woodstock. Thus, from the very first, Winston was a source of trouble to his family.

Winston was born into one of the most distinguished families in Great Britain. His father was Lord Randolph Churchill, third son of the seventh duke of Marlborough. The Churchills had been soldiers and statesmen since the early 1700s, when John Churchill led the armies of Queen Anne to

Blenheim Palace, where Winston Churchill was born into a life of wealth and privilege. His noble blood and aristocratic upbringing served him well later as Britain's prime minister.

An Early Arrival

Winston Churchill was born two months ahead of schedule. After the birth, his father, Lord Randolph Churchill, wrote this letter to Jennie's mother. It is found in Winston S. Churchill, *the biography written by Randolph Churchill, Winston's son.*

"I have just time to write a line, to send by the London Dr [doctor] tell you that all has up to now thank God gone off very well with my darling Jennie. She had a fall on Tuesday walking with the shooters, & a rather imprudent & rough drive in a pony carriage brought on the pains on Saturday night. We tried to stop them, but it was no use. They went on all Sunday. Of course the Oxford physician cld [could] not come. We telegraphed for the London man Dr Hope but he did not arrive till this morning. The country Dr is however a clever man, & the baby was safely born at 1.30 this morning after about 8 hrs labour. She suffered a good deal poor darling, but was vy [very] plucky & had no chloroform. The boy is wonderfully pretty so everybody says dark eyes and hair & vy healthy considering its prematureness. My mother & Clementine [Randolph's aunt] have been everything to Jennie, & she cld not be more comfortable. We have just got a most excellent nurse & wet nurse coming down this afternoon & please God all will go vy well with both. . . . I hope the baby things will come with all speed. We have to borrow some from the Woodstock Solicitor's wife."

victory over the French. The grateful queen made Churchill the first duke of Marlborough and built him a fabulous palace, Blenheim, named for his greatest battle.

Winston's mother Jennie was a beautiful American, daughter of wealthy New York businessman Leonard Jerome. Her ancestors, likewise, had been soldiers, serving with George Washington during the American Revolution.

Churchill was to lead a life of luxury, power, and privilege. Servants would wait on him from childhood on—dressing him, running his bathwater, serving his meals. His family name, his parents' status, would open many doors in later life.

He had every advantage except one— the affection and attention of his mother and father. It was normal for upper-class parents to spend little time with their children, but "the neglect and lack of [interest in Winston] shown by his parents were remarkable, even judged by the standards of late Victorian and Edwardian days."[7] Lord Randolph was too busy with politics. Many thought he might be prime minister someday. Jennie was too busy with clothes, parties, and what she later called "a whirl of gaieties and excitement."[8]

From the time he was one month old, Winston was cared for by a nanny (nurse), Elizabeth Anne Everest. He called her "Woom," his early attempt at saying the word "woman." "Mrs. Everest it was who looked after me and tended all my wants," he later wrote. "It was to her I poured out my many troubles, both now and in my schooldays."[9] He loved her dearly and kept her picture in his bedroom all his life. His only other companion as a child was Jack, a brother six years younger, with whom he had little in common.

Jennie, Churchill's mother, was the daughter of a wealthy New York businessman. Preoccupied with parties and clothes, she had little time for young Churchill.

Love at a Distance

Though Lord Randolph and Jennie mostly ignored him, Winston adored his parents. His mother "shone for me like the Evening Star. I loved her dearly—but at a distance."[10] His father was his hero. He later memorized Lord Randolph's speeches, copied his speaking style and posture, and—when he reached Parliament—sat in his father's old seat.

The resentment young Winston might have felt toward his parents was directed at others. "I was," he wrote, "what grown-up people in their off-hand way called a 'troublesome boy.'"[11] He resisted any kind of authority. He ordered servants about as if they were slaves. His dancing teacher called him "the naughtiest small boy in the world."[12]

Such an attitude was bound to create trouble in school. In November 1882, Winston was sent to St. James's boarding school. It was run by a cruel headmaster who beat his students' bare flesh with a wooden switch. Beatings were not unusual in British schools, but, as Churchill wrote, "I am sure no . . . boy of my day, ever received such a cruel flogging as this Headmaster was accustomed to inflict upon the little boys who were in his care and power."[13]

Churchill was flogged often, probably with cause. A student at St. James in later years wrote:

> Dreadful legends were told about Winston Churchill, who had been taken away from the school. His naughtiness appeared to have surpassed anything. He had been flogged for taking sugar from the pantry, and so far from being penitent [apologetic], he had taken the Headmaster's sacred straw hat

The seven-year-old Churchill stares at the camera with a self-assured, arrogant air. A disobedient and strong-willed child, Churchill was continually reprimanded for his unruly behavior.

A Constant Troublemaker

The following year was better. There was good progress in history, geography, writing, and spelling. Concerning Churchill's conduct, however, the headmaster wrote, "Very bad—is a constant trouble to everybody and is always in some scrape or other."[17] The truth was that Churchill made an effort only in the subjects that interested him. He admitted as much later, writing, "My teachers . . . were offended. They had large resources of compulsion at their disposal, but I was stubborn. Where my reason, imagination or interest were not engaged, I would not or I could not learn."[18]

He wrote his parents he was happy at St. James's. He was anything but happy. "How I hated this school," he later wrote, "and what a life of anxiety I lived there for more than two years."[19] The truth came out during a visit home. Woom undressed him and found his back and buttocks covered with scars from the whippings he had received. Jennie promptly removed him from St. James's and enrolled him at a school run by two sisters in Brighton.

As grim as the experiences at St. James's were, they may have helped strengthen Churchill's character. The stubbornness that infuriated his teachers would be a virtue years later when he, alone, warned his country about the threat of Hitler. And his son Randolph wrote:

> His parents kept him at a distance and this, combined with his mutinous outlook at school, early compelled him to stand on his own feet and to make his way in the world by his own exertions and by his own methods. He had to

from where it hung over the door and kicked it to pieces. His sojourn at this school had been one long feud with authority.[14]

His grades were almost as bad as his conduct. In December, Jennie wrote to Randolph, "As to Winston's improvement I am sorry to say I see none. . . . Altogether I am disappointed."[15] At the end of the term, he was at the bottom of his class. His report read, "He will do well, but must treat his work in general more seriously next Term."[16]

fight every inch of his road thru life. . . .
To achieve success he had to develop
that intense power of concentration
which, as it grew, was to serve him and
his fellow countrymen so well.[20]

Winston's four years at Brighton were
far happier. "At this school I was allowed to
learn things which interested me: French,
History, lots of Poetry by heart, and above
all Riding and Swimming."[21] Churchill began to read the books of Robert Louis
Stevenson and Rider Haggard. He read
newspapers and began to take an interest in
politics, particularly in his father's career.

Under the British system, the leaders
of the political party that has a majority in
the House of Commons (one of the two
houses of Parliament) become the ministers (chief officers) of the government.
The head of the party in power is the
prime minister. Lord Randolph now was
one of the leading figures in the Conservative Party. When the Conservatives won a
majority in 1886, Randolph was made
chancellor of the exchequer (so called because money had been counted out on a
checkered tablecloth in medieval times).
The chancellor of the exchequer is head
of the treasury and the second most powerful man in the British government.

Randolph was ambitious. Wanting to
replace Lord Salisbury as prime minister,
he drew up a budget that would cut military spending. Salisbury rejected the plan,
however, and Randolph decided to resign
in protest. He thought other Conservatives
would join him, Salisbury would be forced
to resign, and that he would be chosen the
new Conservative leader and thus become
prime minister. This did not happen, and
because of Randolph's miscalculation, his
political influence was over.

Churchill during his years at Brighton. Brighton
suited Churchill much better than had St. James,
and he tried harder at his studies.

Randolph's health was failing, as well.
He had entered the final stage of a sexu-
ally transmitted disease known as syphilis,
contracted many years earlier as a student
at Oxford. As a prank, some fellow students got young Randolph drunk and
took him to a prostitute, from whom he
caught the disease.

In terminal syphilis the brain is slowly
destroyed. The victim experiences paralysis and loss of speech, and acts irrationally.
Lord Randolph had suffered his first attack of paralysis in 1881. His violent shifts
of mood and even his treatment of Winston may have been due to his illness.

A Fear of Examinations

With no knowledge of his father's condition, Winston was studying, hoping to be accepted into Harrow, one of Britain's best "public schools." (A British public school is the equivalent of a private prep school in the United States.) For once, he worked hard in preparation for the entrance examination, which he took in March 1888. He dreaded exams, however, and later wrote:

I should have liked to say what I knew. They [teachers] always tried to ask what I did not know. When I would have willingly displayed my knowledge, they sought to expose my ignorance. This sort of treatment had only one result: I did not do well in examinations. [22]

The exam, in this case, was to translate passages in Latin and Greek into English. Churchill went absolutely blank. He did little except write his name at the top of the page. To his amazement, he was accepted at Harrow, but it was because of

A Product of His Time

Although Churchill was one of the most forward-thinking men of the twentieth century, his view of the British Empire was grounded in the 1800s. He explained this in the preface to his book My Early Life.

"When I survey this work as a whole I find I have drawn a picture of a vanished age. The character of society, the foundations of politics, the methods of war, the outlook of youth, the scale of values, are all changed, and changed to an extent I should not have believed possible in so short a space without any violent domestic revolution. I cannot pretend to feel that they are in all respects changed for the better. I was a child of the Victorian era, when the structure of our country seemed firmly set, when its position in trade and on the seas was unrivalled, and when the realisation of the greatness of our Empire and of our duty to preserve it was ever growing stronger. In those days the dominant forces in Great Britain were very sure of themselves and of their doctrines. They thought they could teach the world the art of government, and the science of economics. They were sure they were supreme at sea and consequently safe at home. They rested therefore sedately under the conviction of power and security. Very different is the aspect of these anxious and dubious times."

A Teacher's Report

Until he attended Sandhurst, Britain's military academy, Churchill's scholastic career could hardly be called successful. In 1888 his housemaster at Harrow, H.O.D. Davidson, wrote to Churchill's mother that he was allowing Winston permission for a short visit home during his first term. The letter is found in Winston S. Churchill *by his son, Randolph Churchill.*

"I have decided to allow Winston to have his exeat [permission to leave school]: but I must own that he has not deserved it. I do not think . . . that he is in any way *willfully* troublesome: but his forgetfulness, carelessness, unpunctuality, and irregularity in every way, have really been so serious, that I write to ask you, when he is home to speak very gravely to him on the subject. When a boy first comes to a public school, one always expects a certain amount of helplessness. . . . But a week or two is generally enough for a boy to get used to the ways of the place. Winston, I am sorry to say, has, if anything got worse as the term passed. Constantly late for school, losing his books, and papers, and various other things into which I need not enter—he is so regular in his irregularity, that I really don't know what to do: and sometimes think he cannot help it. But if he is unable to conquer this slovenliness [disorder], (for I think all the complaints I have to make of him can be grouped under this head, though it takes various forms); he will never make a success of public school. . . . As far as ability goes he ought to be at the top of his form [class], whereas he is at the bottom. Yet I do not think he is idle: only his energy is fitful, and when he gets to his work it is generally too late for him to do it well. . . . He is a remarkable boy in many ways, and it would be a thousand pities if such good abilities were made useless by habitual negligence."

the Churchill name, not because of his performance on the entrance exam.

At Harrow, Winston was at the bottom of his class. As before, he learned only what interested him. He did, however, develop a feel for the English language and began to realize that he could write well. He made a bargain with a fellow student.

He wrote his friend's essays in exchange for Latin translations.

His parents still ignored him. At both Brighton and Harrow, his letters home were full of requests for his mother and father to visit him. Lord Randolph once came to Brighton on business but did not take the trouble to visit his twelve-year-old son. "I cannot think why you did not come to see me, while you were in Brighton," Winston wrote his father. "I was very disappointed but I suppose you were too busy to come."[23] "I do hope both you & Mama will come as last Speech day nobody came to see me & it was vy [very] dull," he wrote from Harrow in 1889. "I shall be awfully disappointed if you don't come."[24] Nobody came.

Lord Randolph had given some thought, but not much, to what would become of his son. Years before, watching Winston play with his huge army of toy soldiers, he had asked if Winston would like to go into the army. Churchill later wrote:

I thought it would be splendid to command an Army, so I said "Yes" at once: and immediately I was taken at my word. For years I thought my father with his experience and flair had discerned in me the qualities of military

No Head for Figures

Mathematics was never one of Churchill's stronger subjects, and it was to show later when he was Britain's chief financial officer, the chancellor of the exchequer. In My Early Life, *he recounted his first encounters with math.*

"We continued to toil every day, not only at letters, but at words, and also at what was much worse, figures. Letters after all had only got to be known, and when they stood together in a certain way one recognized their formation and that it meant a certain sound or word which one uttered when pressed sufficiently. But the figures were tied into all sorts of tangles and did things to one another which it was extremely difficult to forecast with complete accuracy. You had to say what they did each time they were tied up together, and the Governess apparently attached enormous importance to the answer being exact. If it was not right, it was wrong. It was not any use being 'nearly right.' In some cases these figures got into debt with one another; you had to borrow one or carry one, and afterwards you had to pay back the one you had borrowed. These complications cast a steadily gathering shadow over my life. . . . They became a general worry and preoccupation. More especially was this true when we descended into dismal bog called 'sums.' There appeared to be no limit to these. When one sum was done, there was always another. Just as soon as I managed to tackle a particular class of these afflictions, some other much more variegated [different] type was thrust upon me."

genius. But I was told later that he had only come to the conclusion that I was not clever enough to go to the Bar [a legal career].[25]

Accordingly, Churchill was enrolled in the Army Class at Harrow—the group of boys whose goal was Sandhurst, Britain's military academy. To enter Sandhurst, however, it was necessary to achieve a certain score on an exam. Winston failed the exam twice—this time, even his family name did not help. After extensive tutoring, though, he barely passed on the third try. He would enter Sandhurst in 1893, 92nd in a class of 102.

Churchill thought his father would be proud of him. Once more he was disappointed. Cadets were given the choice of which branch of the army to serve. The infantry was the most popular branch, but Churchill's low class standing meant he would train instead for the cavalry, a more expensive proposition, since a cavalry officer was expected to provide and maintain his own horses. Instead of congratulating his son, Lord Randolph wrote an extraordinary letter, saying "I no longer attach the slightest weight to anything you may say about your own acquirements & exploits."[26]

This letter was the product of an increasingly disturbed mind. In the final stages of his fatal disease, Lord Randolph's periods of sanity were more infrequent. In 1894, on the advice of doctors, he and Jennie went on a lengthy cruise. "I never saw him again," Churchill wrote, "except as a swiftly fading shadow."[27] On January 24, 1895, a month after his return, Lord Randolph died.

Churchill suffered another loss in June when his nanny, Woom, died. He was at her bedside, holding her hand. "She had been my dearest and most intimate friend during the whole of the twenty years I had lived," he wrote.[28]

In the meantime, Churchill had finally found something to which he could devote his full attention. He started Sandhurst in the "Awkward Squad"—cadets who needed extra work—but soon began to improve. "I was no longer handicapped by past neglect of Latin, French, or Mathematics," he wrote. "We had now to learn fresh things and we all started equal. Tactics, Fortifications, Topography (mapmaking), Military Law and Military Administration form the whole curriculum."[29]

Churchill loved it all, especially riding, and he finished second in the school-wide

Churchill in the uniform of the Fourth Hussars. During his years in training for the cavalry, Churchill thought he had found the career for which he was ideally suited.

Churchill and Religion

Churchill lived in a time when an increasing number of scientific discoveries and theories seemed to contradict the traditional teachings of Christianity. He saw no conflict and, indeed, thought science and religion could and should exist together, as he explained in My Early Life.

"I could not feel that the Supreme Creator who gave us our minds as well as our souls would be offended if they did not always run smoothly together in double harness. After all He must have foreseen this from the beginning and of course He would understand it all.

Accordingly I have always been surprised to see some of our Bishops and clergy making such heavy weather about reconciling the Bible story with modern scientific and historical knowledge. Why do they want to reconcile them? If you are the recipient of a message which cheers your heart and fortifies your soul, which promises you reunion with those you have loved in a world of larger opportunity and wider sympathies, why should you worry about the shape or colour of the travel-stained envelope; whether it is duly stamped, whether the date on the postmark is right or wrong? These matters may be puzzling, but they are certainly not important. What is important is the message and the benefits to you of receiving it. Close reasoning can conduct one to the precise conclusion that miracles are impossible . . . and at the same time one may rejoice to read how Christ turned the water into wine in Cana of Galilee or walked on the lake or rose from the dead. . . . The idea that nothing is true except what we comprehend is silly, and that ideas which our minds cannot reconcile are mutually destructive, sillier still. . . . I therefore adopted quite early in life a system of believing whatever I wanted to believe, while at the same time leaving reason to pursue unfettered whatever paths she was capable of treading."

contest. He learned to ride in competitions and to play polo. He was popular with other cadets. He did well in all his subjects and, late in 1894, graduated 8th in his class of 150. In March 1895, he became Second Lieutenant Winston Churchill of Her Majesty's Fourth Hussars. "I passed out of Sandhurst and into the world," he wrote. "It opened [before me] like Aladdin's cave."[30]

2 Soldier, Writer, Politician

The Fourth Hussars were stationed at Aldershot, about fifty miles southwest of London. Churchill's duties were light. In fact, he was bored. "The more I see of soldiering," he wrote Jennie after only five months in the army, "the more I like it, but the more I feel convinced that it is not my *métier* [calling]. Well, we shall see."[31]

Politics was what fired his imagination. He had followed his father's career since childhood, meeting and talking with the leading political figures of the time at his parents' house. Now, only a few months after his father's death, he was determined to take up where Lord Randolph had left off.

Before entering politics, however, he needed to make a name for himself, and one way to do it was as a soldier. Aldershot, however, provided few opportunities for glory. Therefore Churchill looked for action, and first found it in Cuba, where Spain was attempting to put down a revolt. Through an old friend of his father's, he managed to get permission to go as an observer. He also talked a London newspaper, the *Daily Graphic*, into paying him for the articles written from the front. This would be the start of a long career as a writer.

On November 2, 1895, he sailed with another officer for New York, spent a week there entertained in grand style by friends of Jennie's, then went on to Havana, Cuba. For two weeks he marched through the forests with Spanish troops, who were constantly under fire from the rebels. It was Churchill's first experience in combat, and he found it thrilling. "There is nothing more exhilarating than to be shot at without result," he wrote.[32]

In December he returned to England, having written half a dozen articles, some critical of the war. He himself was criticized. "Sensible people," wrote one newspaper, "will wonder what motive could possibly impel a British officer to mix himself up in a dispute with the merits of which he had absolutely nothing to do. . . . Spending a holiday fighting other people's battles is rather an extraordinary proceeding even for a Churchill."[33]

Resolved to Learn

The chance of more action lay just ahead, for the Fourth Hussars were sent to India. Arriving in the fall of 1896, the regiment was assigned to Bangalore in the far south of the country. For some time, there was no action. In fact, some officers spent most of their time sleeping.

Not Churchill. His mind was too active for such laziness, and he was increasingly aware of how slight his education had been. Later, he wrote:

Churchill's Advice to Youth

Churchill possessed boundless energy, ambition, and faith in his own abilities. These show in the advice he gave to young men in My Early Life, *written after World War I.*

"Come on now all you young men, all over the world. You are needed more than ever now to fill the gap of a generation shorn [depleted] by the war. You have not an hour to lose. You must take your places in Life's fighting line. Twenty to twenty-five! These are the years! Don't be content with things as they are. 'The earth is yours and the fullness thereof.' Enter upon your inheritance, accept your responsibilities. Raise the glorious flags again, advance them upon the new enemies, who constantly gather upon the front of the human army, and have only to be assaulted to be overthrown. Do not take No for an answer. Never submit to failure. Don't be fobbed off [pacified] with mere personal success or acceptance. You will make all kinds of mistakes; but as long as you are generous and true, and also fierce, you cannot hurt the world or even seriously distress her. She was made to be wooed and won by youth. She has lived and thrived only by repeated subjugations."

I resolved to read history, philosophy, economics, and things like that; and I wrote to my mother asking for such books as I heard of on these topics. She responded with alacrity [speed], and every month mail brought me a substantial package of what I thought were standard works. In history, I decided to begin with Edward Gibbon [author of a major historical examination of the Roman Empire]. . . . All through the long glistening middle hours of the Indian day, from when we quitted stables till the evening shadows proclaimed the hour of Polo, I devoured Gibbon.[34]

In 1897 Churchill went home on leave. While in London he visited the offices of the conservative party and said he wanted to run for Parliament. No seats were vacant at the time, but the party arranged for him to make his first political speech, on June 26, just outside the city of Bath. He told an enthusiastic audience that British workers had "more to hope for from the rising tide of Tory [Conservative] Democracy than from the dried-up drainpipe of Radicalism [the liberals]." He ended with a blast at those who said the British Empire was in decline:

Do not believe these croakers, but give the lie to their dismal croaking by showing by our actions that the vigour and vitality of our race [nation] is unimpaired and that our determination is to uphold the Empire that we have inherited from our fathers as Englishmen, that our flag shall fly high upon the sea, our voice be heard in the councils of Europe, our Sovereign [Queen Victoria] supported by the love of her subjects, then we shall continue to pursue that course marked out for us by an all-wise hand and carry out our mission of bearing peace, civilisation and good government to the uttermost ends of the earth.[35]

A few days later, Churchill learned that a British force was being organized to put down a revolt in northern India. He was determined to be part of it. Luckily, the troops were to be commanded by General Bindon Blood, whom Churchill had met the year before. He now telegraphed Blood, reminding the general that he had promised to take Churchill with him if he were to lead troops into action. Blood, who had been impressed by the young Hussar, responded that while there were no vacancies for officers, Churchill could come as a correspondent.

He returned to Bangalore, and, after obtaining permission from his regimental commander, traveled two thousand miles through the summer heat to Malakand, near the Afghanistan border. When his train arrived, the first week in September, he learned that his mother had arranged for a London newspaper to publish his letters from the front. Churchill's relationship with his mother had changed dramatically. Jennie now found her son more interesting and did everything she could to help his career. She was still young and beautiful. She had several lovers, before and after her husband's death, including Queen Victoria's son—Albert Edward, Prince of Wales. She used her influence with prominent men to help her son.

Getting Away with Everything

It was unusual—especially for so young an officer—to be able to go here and there in search of action. And for an officer on active service to be a newspaper correspondent as well was unheard of. Churchill got away with it through his family name, his mother's influence, and his own brashness. Others might follow the rules or go through channels; Churchill, when he wanted something, would go right to the top, and he usually went where he pleased and did what he wanted.

Churchill (second row, far left) with members of his squadron's football team. At this time, Churchill was traveling the world, attempting to participate in British military campaigns.

A Romantic View of War

When Churchill was a young lieutenant in the last years of the nineteenth century, war was a thrilling adventure. Writing after World War I in My Early Life, *he deplored what warfare had become.*

"It is a shame that war should have flung all this [glamour] aside in its greedy, base [degraded], opportunistic march, and should turn instead to chemists in spectacles, and chauffeurs pulling levers of aeroplanes or machine guns. . . . War, which used to be cruel and magnificent, has now become cruel and squalid. In fact it has been completely spoilt. It is all the fault of Democracy and Science. From the moment that either of these meddlers and muddlers was allowed to take part in actual fighting, the doom of War was sealed. Instead of a small number of well-trained professionals championing their country's cause with ancient weapons and a beautiful intricacy of archaic manoeuvre, sustained at every moment by the applause of their nation, we now have entire populations, including even women and children, pitted against one another in brutish mutual extermination, and only a set of blear-eyed clerks left to add up the butcher's bill. From the moment Democracy was admitted to, or rather forced itself upon the battlefield, War ceased to be a gentleman's game."

He wanted action, and he got plenty of it. On September 16, 1897, he and a small band of soldiers were separated from the main body of troops in the Malmund valley. "All of a sudden," he wrote:

The whole hillside began to be spotted with smoke, and tiny figures descended every moment nearer toward us. . . . The targets were too tempting to be resisted. I borrowed the Martini [rifle] of the [soldier] by whom I lay. He was quite content to hand me cartridges. I began to shoot carefully at the men gathering in the rocks. A lot of bullets whistled about us. But we lay very flat, and no harm was done. [36]

Churchill's first book, *The Story of the Malakand Field Force*, was published in 1898. It was a success in Britain. Nine months after its publication it had earned for its author more than he had earned in four years as an army officer. The prime minister Lord Salisbury, invited him to the official residence at Number 10 Downing Street. The Prince of Wales wrote him, "I cannot resist writing a few lines to congratulate you on the success of your book! . . . Everybody is reading it, and I only hear it spoken of with praise." [37]

Senior officers, however, despised both the author and the book, which they called "A Subaltern's [junior officer's] Hints to Generals."[38] Churchill was getting a bad reputation in the army as an adventurer, a medal hunter. This was certainly true. His goal was a seat in Parliament, and he thought he would have a better chance as a war hero. He wrote his mother that his bravery in battle was "Foolish, perhaps, but I play for high stakes and given an audience there is no act too daring or too noble" and "I should like to come back and wear my medals at some big dinner or other function."[39]

One officer who thoroughly disapproved of Churchill was General Lord Herbert Kitchener, who was leading British troops in an effort to recapture the Sudan, an African country just south of Egypt. His campaign was reaching its climax in 1898, and Churchill desperately wanted to be there.

Friends in High Places

Churchill and Jennie tried everything to obtain a place for him in the African campaign, but Kitchener absolutely refused. Finally, after the intervention of the prime minister, the Prince of Wales, and the War Office, Kitchener gave in. Churchill was as-

Churchill's reputation as a medal hunter impeded his being assigned an appointment with British troops in Africa. With the intervention of his mother, however, Churchill joined the campaign and earned the respect of all who worked with him. He is pictured here during the Africa campaign (back row, second from left).

signed to the Twenty-first Lancers as a "supernumerary [extra] lieutenant." He quickly left London, arranging for the *Morning Post* to pay him as a correspondent.

In the Sudan, as in India, Churchill distinguished himself both as a soldier and as a reporter. He fought bravely, winning even Kitchener's admiration. During the final engagement, the Battle of Omdurman, he had the good luck to take part in the last cavalry charge in British military history—and the better luck to live through it, for many of his comrades were killed.

Churchill's articles were critical of the army. His second book, *The River War,* was especially critical of Kitchener for ordering the tomb of Mahdi [the native leader who had defeated the British in 1885] opened and the corpse's head cut off to serve as an example to others who might consider challenging Britain.

Churchill now intended to resign from the army and run for Parliament. Conservative Party officials told him that a "safe" seat, a district in which the voters of one party are numerous enough to guarantee election of that party's candidate, would require a sizable cash donation. Under the British system, it is not necessary to live in the area one represents in Parliament. The leading men in a party—and those willing to contribute handsomely—run in safe seats.

Churchill could not afford a safe seat but was determined to run, anyway. Upon resigning from the army in 1899, he became a Conservative Party candidate in Oldham, a working-class district in northwest England. The Conservatives were not strong in Oldham, but Churchill fought a spirited campaign. He wrote a friend, "I shall never forget the succession of great halls packed with excited people until there was not room for one single person more—speech after speech—meeting after meeting three even four in one night—intermittent flashes of Heat & Light & enthusiasm—with cold air and the rattle of a carriage in between."[40] It was like the old days for Jennie, who came to campaign for him on election day dressed entirely in blue, the Conservative Party color.

It wasn't enough. He lost by 1,293 votes out of 48,672 cast. Despite the loss, he had been impressive. A future Conservative prime minister, Arthur Balfour, wrote him, "I hope, however, you will not be discouraged."[41] Churchill was anything but discouraged. There was another war in the making.

The Boer War

This time, the scene was South Africa, where the British and the Dutch had long been hostile competitors. After many tense years, the Dutch settlers, or Boers (from a Dutch word meaning "farmer"), went inland, forming their own country known as the Transvaal. The British annexed the Transvaal in 1877, but the Boers fought back and, in 1881, defeated the British. The British, although not granting complete independence, agreed to let the Boers run their own affairs.

When gold was discovered in Transvaal in 1886, hundreds of foreigners, many of them British, poured into the region, threatening to take over. The Boers tried to limit the power of these *Uitlanders* ["foreigners"]. British troops moved to the border between the British Cape Colony and the Transvaal. The Boers sent an ultimatum, demanding the withdrawl of the troops. The British refused, and war was declared in October 1899.

English troops during the Boer War. Initially thinking that the war would be a limited engagement, British troops became bogged down in South Africa for years.

The British estimated that the war against the Boers, who had no organized army, would last only about three months. Churchill's greatest fear was that he would arrive too late. By now, he had a large following as a reporter and author, and the *Morning Post* had agreed to pay him a thousand pounds sterling (£1,000) for four months. (The amount in nineteenth-century British currency is the equivalent of about $40,000 today.)

Churchill needed every penny. He was not a rich man. His father had left many debts, and his mother was as extravagant as always. Churchill, also, was accustomed to living in style, usually more style than he could afford. "Winston is a man of simple tastes," his good friend F.E. Smith once said. "He is always prepared to put up with the best of everything."[42]

When his ship arrived at Cape Town on October 31, Churchill discovered that he need not have worried about missing the war. The British had not won a single battle. The Boers had surrounded two British towns and were threatening a third, Ladysmith.

Churchill went to the town of Durban and there met an old friend, Captain Aylmer Haldane. Haldane, who was taking some troops on an armored train toward Ladysmith on November 15 to test the Boers' strength, suggested that Churchill come along. Another reporter tried to talk him out of it, but Churchill said, "I have a feeling, a sort of intuition, that if I go something will come of it."[43]

A train covered with iron plates, with slits through which guns might be fired, was a new idea. It turned out to be a terrible idea, as well. All an enemy had to do was wait until the train went by, then set off an explosion under it.

Churchill as a war correspondent in the Boer War. Captured during the campaign, Churchill made a daring escape.

That was exactly what the Boers did, derailing the cars at the rear of the train and then attacking it. As bullets whizzed around him, Churchill immediately took charge and organized the soldiers in clearing the tracks so the engine and front cars could carry some of the troops out of danger. Churchill, however, was not among them. He wrote:

> Suddenly on the other side of the railway . . . I saw a horseman galloping furiously, a tall, dark figure, holding his rifle in his right hand. He pulled up his horse almost in its own length [evidence of an excellent horse]. . . . The animal stood stock still, so did he, and so did I. I looked toward the river, I looked toward the plate-layer's hut. The Boer continued to look along his sights. I thought there was absolutely no chance of escape, if he fired he would surely hit me, so I held up my hands and surrendered myself [as] a prisoner of war. [44]

Churchill in Prison

Churchill and the other Britons were imprisoned in the Boer capital of Pretoria. Churchill claimed that as a correspondent, he should be released. The Boers, however, had seen him directing the soldiers and, upon learning that he was first cousin of a British duke, decided he was a prize worth keeping.

They didn't keep him long. On December 12, 1899, Churchill, Haldane, and another prisoner tried to escape by climbing over a wall. Churchill went first and got over unseen, but the other two were spotted by sentries before they could make it.

Mind Over Matter

Churchill's physical stamina and his great courage are remarkable when one considers that he was not a physically strong person. Anthony Storr, in his contribution to Churchill Revised, *coauthored with A.J.P. Taylor and others, suggests that Churchill deliberately made himself other than he really was.*

"His massive head, the small size of his chest compared with his abdomen, the rounded contours of his body, and the small size of his extremities were all characteristic [of a person not inclined to physical activity]. So was his smooth, soft skin, which was so delicate that he always wore specially obtained silk underwear. One would expect a man with his physique to be . . . earthy, unhurried, deliberate, and predictable. . . . Churchill was a very much more aggressive and dominant individual than one would expect from his basic physique. His love of risk, of physical adventure, his energy and assertiveness are traits which were . . . unexpected in a man of Churchill's structure. In other words, we have a picture of a man who was, to a marked extent, forcing himself to go against his own inner nature: a man who was neither naturally strong, nor naturally particularly courageous, but who made himself both in spite of his temperamental and physical endowment. The more one examines Winston Churchill as a person, the more one is forced to the conclusion that his aggressiveness, his courage, and his dominance were not rooted in his inheritance, but were the product of deliberate decision and iron will."

Churchill's remarkable personal characteristics overcame the fact that he was not a very strong man physically. His determination, daring, and calm in the face of obstacles allowed him to accomplish remarkable things.

Churchill was alone, without a map, a compass, or money. He also lacked any knowledge of Afrikaans, the Boer language.

He did have, however, a huge amount of daring. He calmly walked through the streets of Pretoria and into the countryside. He wandered about for a day and a half and finally, exhausted, knocked at the door of a house, hoping that it might belong to one of the few Englishmen still living in the Transvaal.

The door was answered by a tall man holding a pistol. In Afrikaans, he asked Churchill what he wanted. In English, Churchill explained who he was. The man, John Howard, took him inside, closed the door, and said, "Thank God you have come here! It is the only house for twenty miles where you would not have been handed over. But we are all British here, and we will see you through!"[45]

Howard and a handful of other Englishmen hid Churchill at the bottom of a mine shaft and, after several days, hid him in the middle of a railway car loaded with sacks of wool, headed east to Portuguese East Africa (present Mozambique). When he arrived there safely, Churchill jumped out of his hiding place—covered with coal dust—shouted with joy, fired his pistol

Churchill (on horse) after his escape from the Boers on December 12, 1899. Churchill's story of his capture and escape thrilled Britons, who were growing increasingly disappointed over the lack of success in South Africa.

The First Defeat

Churchill first attempted to win a seat in Parliament in the working-class town of Oldham in 1899. He campaigned hard but made several mistakes, including speaking against one of his own party's bills, and was beaten by about 1,300 votes. In My Early Life, *he wrote about the defeat.*

"Then came the recriminations which always follow every kind of defeat. Everyone threw the blame on me. I have noticed that they nearly always do. I supposed it is because they think I shall be able to bear it best. Mr [Arthur] Balfour, then leader of the House of Commons, on hearing that I had declared against his Clerical Tithes Bill, said in the Lobby [outside the House chamber], quite justifiably I must admit, 'I thought he was a young man of promise, but it appears he is a young man of promises.' Party newspapers wrote leading articles to say what a mistake it was to entrust the fighting of great working-class constituencies to young inexperienced candidates, and everyone then made haste to pass away from a dismal incident. I returned to London with those feelings of deflation which a bottle of champagne or even soda-water represents when it has been half emptied and left uncorked for a night."

twice into the air, and headed for the British consulate.

Churchill's escape caused a sensation. His adventure was a bright light in an otherwise gloomy time of British defeats. He returned to Durban, where he was met by blaring bands and a cheering crowd. In Britain, he was famous. London newspapers were full of his exploits, and people everywhere sang the newest music-hall song:

You've heard of Winston Churchill;
This is all I need to say—
He's the latest and the greatest
Correspondent of the day! [46]

Churchill was offered and accepted a commission as lieutenant in the army but was allowed to continue as a reporter. He rode with the troops that liberated Ladysmith. When the Boers were defeated outside Pretoria, he went to his former prison, tore down the Boer flag, and raised the Union Jack of Great Britain.

The war would drag on for years as the Boers, overwhelmed at last by British numbers, adopted the hit-and-run tactics of guerrilla warfare. Churchill, however, had other battles to fight. The time had come for him to reenter the political arena.

3 Conservative to Liberal

Churchill returned to Britain from South Africa, determined to run again for Parliament. He could not have chosen a better time.

Under the British system, a party that either maintains or wins a majority of seats in the House of Commons in a general election must call another election after a certain period of time. The party in power may, however, call a general election sooner than is required if it thinks it can increase its majority.

This happened in 1900. The Conservative Party government had been blamed for early defeats in the Boer War and had lost seats to Liberals in by-elections—votes held to fill vacancies caused by death or retirement. Now, with the war going their way, the Tories decided to try to ride a wave of patriotism sweeping Britain.

A Hardfought Campaign

Churchill was a hero. Eleven constituencies (districts from which members were elected) asked him to be their candidate. He wanted to erase the memory of the preceding year's defeat, however, and returned to Oldham.

The campaign was hardfought. Churchill needed all his fame, the financial backing of the Marlborough family, and the help of some of the leading Tories—such as chancellor of the exchequer Joseph Chamberlain—to squeak through. He won by twenty-two votes.

When the new House of Commons met in January of 1901, the Conservatives had a solid majority of 134 seats. Churchill, however, wasn't there. Members of Parliament received no salary, and Churchill, to get enough money to live on, had gone on a lecture tour. At this time, before radio, television, and movies, public lectures were a prime source of entertainment.

Churchill gave thirty lectures on the Boer War in the month after the election, earning five times the yearly income of a professional man his age. He extended the tour to the United States and Canada. At the end of the series, he was able to write his mother, "I am very proud of the fact that there is not one person in a million who, at the age of twenty-six could have earned £10,000 without any capital in less than two years."[47]

First Speech in Parliament

Early in February 1901, Winston Churchill took his place in Parliament. He wasted very little time in making himself known.

New members usually waited up to a year before making their first speech, but not Churchill. On February 28, the House of Commons first heard the voice that would ring through the chamber for more than half a century.

His subject was the Boer War, which was to continue until 1902. He defended the government, saying that the war had been justified and should be vigorously fought until victory was complete. Then, however, he praised the bravery of the Boers and said that Britain, when the war was over, should treat them generously. This drew frowns from his fellow Tories, most of whom believed the Boers were traitors.

A year before, *Vanity Fair* magazine had published an article on Churchill that said,

Churchill during his run for a Parliament seat in 1900. Since members of Parliament received no salary, Churchill had to miss his first Parliament meeting because he was off earning a living.

"He is ambitious; he means to get on, and he loves his country. But he can hardly be the slave of any party."[48] Churchill's maiden speech demonstrated a streak of independence that would rapidly grow.

He next took up military spending, which had been his father's downfall. When the government proposed to increase the size of the army to three corps, Churchill objected. He thought an arms buildup might lead to a European war. With remarkable foresight, he described such a war:

> A European war cannot be anything but a cruel, heart-rending struggle, which, if we are ever to enjoy the bitter fruits of victory, must demand, perhaps for several years, the whole manhood of the nation. . . . When mighty populations are impelled on each other . . . a European war can only end in the ruin of the vanquished and the scarcely less fatal commercial dislocation and exhaustion of the conquerors. . . . The wars of peoples will be more terrible than the wars of kings.[49]

Churchill grew more and more discontented with the Tories. "They are a class of right honourable Gentlemen," he told the Commons, "all good men, all honest men—who are ready to make great sacrifices for their opinions, but they have no opinions. They are ready to die for the truth, if they only knew what the truth was."[50]

A Break with Conservatives

The final break was over trade. The Conservative leaders, including Balfour and Chamberlain, wanted to tax imported goods to protect those made in Britain. Churchill was committed, instead, to free trade. He rallied other young Tories to his side. He spoke throughout the country against the government's policy. He went so far as to endorse a Liberal candidate in a by-election in 1903.

This was too much for the Conservative Party in Oldham, which voted not to support Churchill in the next election. It was also too much for the government. As he was delivering another speech against the Tories in March 1904, first Balfour, then the members of the cabinet, then all but a handful of Churchill's supporters rose and walked out of the House chamber to indicate their disapproval.

Finally, on May 31, 1904, Churchill

Generous in Victory

As much as Churchill relished a fight, he was the first to extend mercy to a defeated enemy. This generosity immediately got him into trouble with his own political party in Parliament after the Boer War. He described his philosophy in My Early Life, *written after World War I.*

"Here I must confess that all through my life I have found myself in disagreement alternately with both the historic English parties. I have always urged fighting wars and other contentions with might and main till overwhelming victory and then offering the hand of friendship to the vanquished. . . . And not only in South Africa. I thought we ought to have conquered the Irish and then given them Home Rule: that we ought to have starved out the Germans, and then revictualled [reprovisioned] their country; and that after smashing the General Strike [a countrywide labor walkout in 1926], we should have met the grievances of the miners. I always get into trouble because so few people take this line. I was once asked to devise an inscription for a monument in France. I wrote, 'In war, Resolution. In defeat, Defiance. In victory, Magnanimity. In peace, Goodwill.' The inscription was not accepted. It is all the fault of the human brain being made in two halves, only one of which does any thinking, so that we are all right-handed or left-handed; whereas if we were properly constructed we should use our right and left hands with equal force and skill according to circumstances. As it is, those who can win a war well can rarely make a good peace, and those who could make a good peace would never have won the war. It would perhaps be pressing the argument too far to suggest that I could do both."

made a decision in typically dramatic style. He entered the House chamber, bowed to the Speaker's chair, looked to his left at the Conservative benches, then turned abruptly to the right and took a seat among the Liberals.

"I Am a Glowworm"

It has been claimed that Churchill switched parties because he was ambitious and thought he could achieve high office more quickly as a Liberal. Certainly he was ambitious, and he made no attempt to conceal it. "The one thing he did not trouble to disguise," wrote historian A.L. Rowse, "was the superiority of his talents."[51] Another writer called him "brash, assertive, egocentric, wholly absorbed in himself and his career, and unashamedly on the make."[52] He was, however, a man of high principles. He honestly thought that the Conservative Party had moved too far from his personal beliefs. Later in his career, when the Liberals did the same thing,

Fellow member of the Tory Party Arthur Balfour advocated measures to protect Britain from trade exports. Churchill supported free trade.

Churchill would switch parties once more.

His self-confidence was total. When Churchill first met Violet Asquith, daughter of leading Liberal and future prime minister Herbert Asquith, he complained how little he thought he had accomplished in

Faced with continual disagreements with his Conservative Party, Churchill switched parties in 1904 and became a Liberal.

his thirty-two years. Decades later, writing under her married name Bonham Carter, Asquith reported that Churchill also had said, "We are all worms. But I do believe that I am a glowworm."[53]

As Churchill continued to attack the Conservatives, his former colleagues shunned him. Normally, members of Parliament could remain friends whatever their politics.

Churchill, however, was considered a traitor to his class. Old friends ignored him. He was refused membership in an exclusive club. He was no longer invited to houses in which he once had been welcome.

It was during this time that Churchill finished his first important book, a biography of his father. The book, in addition to telling of Lord Randolph's life, says much

The Light of Genius

One of Churchill's greatest friends was Violet Bonham Carter, daughter of Prime Minister Herbert Asquith. In her book Winston Churchill: An Intimate Portrait, *she drew this distinction between Churchill and the other leading political figures with whom she was familiar.*

"I cannot attempt to analyze, still less to transmit, the light of genius. But I will try to set down, as I remember them, some of the differences which struck me at the time between him and all the others. . . . First and foremost he was incalculable. He ran true to no form. There lurked in every thought and word the ambush of the unexpected. I felt also that the impact of life, ideas and even words upon his mind was not only vivid and immediate, but *direct*. Between him and them there was no shock absorber of vicarious [substituted] thought or precedent gleaned either from books or other minds. His relationship with all experience was firsthand. My father and his friends were mostly scholars. . . . In certain fields of thought there was to them 'nothing new under the sun.' But to Winston Churchill everything under the sun was new—seen and appraised as on the first day of Creation. His approach to life was full of ardor [enthusiasm] and surprise. Even the eternal verities [truths] appeared to him to be an exciting personal discovery. (He often seemed annoyed to find that some of them had occurred to other people long ago.) And because they were so new to him he made them shine for me with a new meaning. However familiar his conclusion it had not been reached by any beaten track. His mind had found its own way everywhere."

about Churchill and what he wanted to be. In one passage, he wrote:

> No one could guess beforehand what he was going to say nor how he would say it. No one said the same kind of things, or said them in the same kind of way. He possessed the strange quality . . . of compelling attention and of getting himself talked about. Every word he spoke was studied with interest and apprehension. Each step he took was greeted with a gathering chorus of astonished cries. [54]

A split in the Conservative Party over trade led Balfour to resign as prime minister. The Liberals' leader, Henry Campbell-Bannerman, was asked to form a government. This change in government made a

The Press Takes Notice

In 1901, shortly after he entered the House of Commons, Churchill defended the Conservative government's actions in South Africa in a speech. This account of his speech in the London Daily News *appears in* Churchill: An Intimate Portrait *by Violet Bonham Carter.*

"To [the government's] rescue came Mr. Winston Churchill in what was certainly the ablest speech he has made since his entry into the House. I say 'ablest' because it was a pure debating speech conceived on lines of singular breadth, argued with great acuteness and closeness and now and then with little gestures and tricks of manner—such as bent shoulder and eager, nervous action of the hands—which at moments made one catch one's breath with the thought of how his father looked and spoke. I do not yet find in this young man the depth of character, the great political force that lay behind all his most fantastic adventures. But nothing could be more remarkable than the way in which this youth has slipped into the Parliamentary manner and had flung himself as it were straight into the mid-current of the thoughts and prejudices of the House of Commons. . . . The speech was a happy stroke for his own Parliamentary reputation and for the Government which has he placed under so deep an obligation. It is not exactly pleasing to hear this young man for there are defects of manner, thought and speech which do not commend themselves to the fastidious taste. But it is clear he is going to arrive as his father arrived before him."

In 1908, Churchill was asked to be the president of the Board of Trade by Prime Minister Herbert Asquith. When asked what he wanted to accomplish, Churchill told Asquith that he wanted to help the poor.

general election necessary in 1905. Having been rejected by Oldham, Churchill ran as a Liberal in North Manchester and was elected.

Campbell-Bannerman gave Churchill his first office, that of under-secretary of state in the colonial office, the branch of the government that administered the far-flung British Empire. The secretary of the colonial office, Lord Elgin, was satisfied to leave the running of the office to his energetic young under-secretary. Churchill's first important contribution was made here. He guided a bill through the House of Commons granting self-rule to the Boers instead of treating them like a defeated enemy. This generosity proved crucial during World War I, when the Boers were among Britain's most loyal allies.

In 1908, Campbell-Bannerman resigned because of ill health and Asquith became prime minister. Asquith wished Churchill to be a member of his cabinet and asked him what he would like to accomplish. Churchill replied that he was interested in helping the poor. Asquith made him president of the Board of Trade, a post similar to secretary of commerce in the United States.

At this time, a man appointed to a cabinet post had to seek re-election to Parliament. When Churchill ran in his district in

For the People; Not One of Them

When he became a member of the Liberal Party, Churchill championed the causes of the common man. His personal experience of the lives of the common people, however, was completely lacking, as Violet Bonham Carter revealed in Churchill: An Intimate Portrait.

"It is to Winston Churchill's signal [outstanding] credit that he embraced [social reforms] and worked and fought with all his heart and might to realize them. . . . It was not in principle or theory that he differed from the rank and file of his party. It was the soil from which he had sprung, his personal background, context and experience which made him seem a 'foreign body' among them, and as such, at times (unjustly) suspect. A mistrustful colleague once said warningly to A.G. Gardiner: 'Don't forget that the aristocrat is still there—latent but submerged.' Though he had supported himself by his own tireless industry, he was not acquainted with poverty. As he once said to me, 'I have always had to earn every penny I possessed but there has never been a day in my life when I could not order a bottle of champagne for myself and offer another to a friend.' I do not think it would ever have occurred to him to travel third-class or on an omnibus [public transportation] in order to save money. . . . I doubt if he ever packed his own clothes. It was simpler far to ring a bell, and throughout his life the bells he rung were answered. The late Sir Edward Marsh, his devoted secretary and friend, once told me that until Winston married . . . he had never heard of the existence of such things as 'lodgings' [furnished rooms, rented to tenants]. . . . A leveled world in which such trivial, irksome, sordid cares were universally imposed would have been drab and odious to him."

North Manchester, however, he lost because a large group of Roman Catholics was angry at him for not supporting self-rule for Ireland. It then became necessary for a Liberal member to resign his safe seat in Dundee, Scotland, so that Churchill could be elected there.

Churchill had only recently become truly aware of poverty in Great Britain. He read a book *Poverty: A Study in Town Life*, and said it "has fairly made my hair stand on end."[55] He learned, among other things, that 30 percent of British children died before reaching the age of five and that living conditions were so bad that half the volunteers for the army in 1900 were rejected as physically unfit.

Churchill set out to improve matters. He was convinced that an increase in the general standard of living would mean more productive workers and more effective soldiers. The answer, he thought, was "the Minimum Standard," a system whereby everyone would be guaranteed a job, a decent salary, and health insurance.

He was not alone. The true leader in the Liberal program of social reform was David Lloyd George, chancellor of the exchequer. Lloyd George, raised by his widowed mother in Wales, knew poverty first hand. He made an odd partner for Churchill, a member of one of Britain's leading families, but, together, they changed their country forever.

Except for Churchill's leadership during World War II, his work with Lloyd George between 1908 and 1912 was the most important, far-reaching part of his career. Their legislation included national health insurance, the eight-hour workday, unemployment insurance, and workplace safety bills. Churchill's dynamic personality was largely responsible for pushing these measures, the foundation of the modern British welfare state, through Parliament. It was "a striking illustration of how much the personality of the Minister in a few critical months may change the course of social legislation."[56]

Marriage and Family

It was also during this time that Churchill became a family man. In the summer of 1904 he had been introduced to nineteen-year-old Clementine Hozier. "Winston just

Churchill campaigning for reelection in Manchester after becoming president of the Board of Trade. Unfortunately, Churchill's stand on denying Ireland self-rule lost him the election.

stared," Clementine later wrote. "He never uttered one word and was very gauche [rude]."[57] In fact, Churchill's social ineptness was due more to ignorance than to rudeness. He did not know how to talk to young women, how to flatter them. He would much rather talk about himself. He had been in love once before, with Pamela Plowden, a young woman he had met in India, but he was more interested in pursuing a political career than in marriage. Clementine would have better luck than Pamela. She and Churchill were married in 1908.

The Churchills' long life together would be a happy one. They used nicknames for each other in their letters: Winston was "Pig," and Clemmie was "Kat." They likewise bestowed nicknames on their five children. Diana (the "Gold-Cream Kitten") was born in 1909, followed by Randolph ("the Chumbolly") in 1911, Sarah ("the Bumblebee") in 1914, Marigold ("the Duckadilly"), who died of blood poisoning at the age of two in 1918, and Mary ("the Mouse") in 1922.

Churchill, who had experienced an unhappy childhood, spent as much time as possible with his children, determined they would not suffer the same pangs of loneliness. As they grew up, he helped build hideouts and entered into their games. One of their favorite games was "Bear" or "Gorilla," in which Churchill would dress in his oldest clothes and hide behind a tree or bush, springing out to chase whichever child happened to pass by first.

An Unpopular Liberal

Among members of the upper class, who were being taxed to pay for the Liberal reforms, Churchill was one of the most hated men in Britain. His cousin, the duke of Marlborough, refused to speak to him. But, even though rejected by the Conservatives, he was not enthusiastically welcomed by the Liberals. Despite his efforts at reform, he was, after all, a member of the aristocracy.

The Liberals were right to suspect Churchill. There was a vast difference between his liberalism and that of Lloyd George. Asquith's wife wrote:

Churchill married Clementine Hozier in 1908. In contrast to his own upbringing, Churchill was a devoted husband and father.

From Lloyd George [Churchill] was to learn the language of Radicalism. It was Lloyd George's native tongue, but it was not his own, and he spoke it "with a difference." This difference may not have been detected by his audiences but it was recognized by those who knew both the teacher and the pupil. [58]

Churchill believed "in a state of things where a benign [generous] upper class dispensed benefits to an industrious, *bien passant* [docile], and grateful lower class." [59] Lloyd George believed, instead, that real power should be shared equally among the classes. The Liberals and the members of the newly formed Labour Party saw this difference and never fully claimed Churchill as one of their own. They "must become his workmates, but could never be his playmates," Asquith's daughter wrote.[60]

Home Secretary

In 1910, Churchill was appointed home secretary, in charge of most of the internal affairs of Britain. He now was head of the British prison system. Having himself been a prisoner of the Boers, he had sympathy for the inmates and made important reforms, creating work for prisoners, providing entertainment and educational opportunities, and making some crimes punishable by fine instead of prison sentences.

Still he continued to acquire enemies. While he wanted to help the poor, he was opposed to their trying to seize power— for example, by organizing strikes. In November 1910, during a strike in Wales, coal miners smashed shop windows in the town of Tonypandy. Churchill sent three hundred London policemen to put down

Chancellor of the Exchequer David Lloyd George joined forces with Winston Churchill to work for social reform. The two made an odd pair, as Lloyd George knew poverty firsthand, while Churchill had never known true want.

the riots. They did so, but two miners were killed. Workers all over Britain were enraged. In their view, the workers had legitimate grievances and the deaths were a result of Churchill's having acted on behalf of the mine owners. From then on, the Labour Party viewed Churchill as an enemy, and "What about Tonypandy?" became their cry.

On January 3, 1911, a small band of armed anarchists (people who plot to overthrow the government by violence) were trapped by police in a house on London's Sydney Street. Churchill couldn't resist the pull of adventure. "It was such fun," he said later.[61] He hurried to the scene and took personal command of the police. During the course of the gun battle between the two sides, the house caught fire. Churchill refused to allow firefighters to extinguish the blaze, and eventually everyone inside was killed.

Newspaper photographers and newsreel cameramen had captured the sight of Churchill, in top hat and frock coat, directing the police. Tories made fun of him and said this was just another example of his reckless hunger for glory. Many British workers, however, were sympathetic to the anarchists and blamed Churchill for their deaths. To them the Sydney Street disaster was another Tonypandy—Churchill against the common people.

Trouble Abroad

Trouble was also brewing outside the country. For more than a century, Britain had been unchallenged militarily. Now Germany, which had become a world power and wanted more colonies, was offering such a challenge. Britain's navy had been its main source of strength for four hundred years, but the Germans had rapidly increased their shipbuilding.

Asquith and his Liberal government, although they hoped for peace and wanted to limit military spending in favor of social reform, saw the danger. The Royal Navy had grown lazy. It needed an energetic leader. It needed Churchill. In September 1911, Asquith offered him the post of First Lord of the Admiralty, the government minister in charge of the navy. Asquith's daughter wrote:

I was just finishing my tea when [Asquith and Churchill] came in. Looking up, I saw Winston's face a radiance like the sun. "Will you come out for a walk with me at once," he said. "You don't want tea?" . . . "I don't want tea—I don't want anything—anything in the world. Your father has just offered me the Admiralty. . . . Look at the people I have had to deal with so far—Judges and convicts! This is a big thing—the biggest thing that has ever come my way—the chance I should have chosen before all others. I shall pour into it everything I've got."[62]

4 From the Admiralty to the Trenches

When Churchill said he would pour all his energy into his new post as First Lord of the Admiralty, he meant exactly that. He always gave himself entirely to whatever task was at hand. Everything else became secondary. Historian A.L. Rowse wrote that Churchill was, "though a man of many ideas, a man of one idea at a time."[63] Soon, Lloyd George complained that Churchill was "taking less and less interest in home politics," instead wanting to talk only about "his blasted ships."[64] Yet, this singleness of purpose would prove invaluable in the 1940s when the purpose was winning World War II.

As for the "blasted ships," they needed his whole attention. The British navy had grown soft. Many of its ships, and its admirals, too, were old and out of date. Churchill was like a gale at sea. He replaced the First Sea Lord (the highest ranking admiral). He created the Naval War Staff and directed it to make the fleet ready for war. He increased the thickness of battleship hulls and enlarged their guns.

One of his most important changes was the conversion of the fleet from steam power to oil. This gave the ships more speed. He constantly argued that more ships were needed—a dramatic change from his stand against military spending only a few years earlier.

Churchill did not confine himself to ships. He was one of the few men of his time to see the possibilities of the airplane as an offensive weapon, rather than as a mobile, high-altitude observation platform. He created the Royal Naval Air Service and made plans to build a fleet of aircraft that could take off from and land on water. He even invented their name—"seaplanes."

As First Lord, Churchill went everywhere, looked into everything, talked to everyone. During his first two years in office, he spent more than two hundred days on the Admiralty yacht *Enchantress,* inspecting ships and ports on every British coast. A naval magazine wrote, "No First Lord in the history of the Navy has shown himself more practically sympathetic with the conditions of the Lower Deck [ordinary sailors] than Winston Churchill."[65] High-ranking officers were kept on alert twenty-four hours a day. Each morning, Churchill asked them, "What would happen if Germany began war today?"[66]

Proposal for Peace

Throughout his career, Churchill was accused of being too eager for a fight. Historian Robert Rhodes James wrote, "He lived for crisis. He profited from crises.

And when crisis did not exist, he strove to invent it."[67] He knew the horrors of war, however, and tried to prevent the one now looming. In October 1913 he proposed a one-year "Naval Holiday" during which no new ships would be built by either Britain or Germany. When the Germans rejected the idea, Churchill knew war would come.

He did not have long to wait. On June 28, 1914, the heir to the throne of Austria was assassinated in the Serbian capital of Sarajevo. A month later, Austria declared war on Serbia. By August, allies of the two countries had been drawn into the war—the Allies (Britain, France, and Russia) on one side, and the Central Powers (Austria, Germany, and Turkey) on the other. World War I had begun.

Heir to the throne of Austria, Archduke Ferdinand I is assassinated in Sarajevo in 1914. The assassination prompted World War I.

Churchill had seen that the British fleet was ready, and he ordered the fleet to battle stations soon after Austria declared war on Serbia. He acted on his own authority, rather than waiting for Britain's formal entry into the war, to eliminate the possibility of a sneak attack. Lord Grey, the British foreign secretary, later gave Churchill credit "that war found us with a strong Fleet in an exceptionally good state of preparation."[68] And historian Robert Rhodes James wrote:

> It is impossible to think of any of [Churchill's] colleagues in the prewar Liberal Government accomplishing so much—or half so much—in so short a time. This is a point many of his critics have failed to take into account. This was a predominantly pacifist government, notably deficient in men with any practical experience of—and even interest in—naval and military affairs. . . . Within the limits in which he had to work Churchill did a great deal, for which he did not at the time receive adequate credit, and which has been denied to him by some subsequent commentators.[69]

As a result, Britain maintained control of the sea throughout the war. German colonies were defeated, and the Central Powers were blockaded, thus limiting food and weapons that could be brought in. Churchill's years of preparation kept the Germans from ever taking the offensive at sea.

On land, it was a different story. Germany tried to win the war quickly, knowing that it was at a disadvantage at sea and that the Allies had greater resources. The plan was to take Paris with one all-out push, thus defeating France, then turn

As First Lord of the Admiralty, Churchill made sure the British navy was well prepared for World War I.

east and capture the Russian capital as well. Britain, Germany thought, would then come to terms.

It almost worked. The Germans poured through Belgium into northern France.

They came within twenty-five miles of Paris but were pushed back by the French and British at the Marne River. The Germans now marched toward the English Channel, trying to circle around the Allies. The Allies pursued them, hoping to cut them off.

The Defense of Antwerp

The Germans' goal was the important Belgian city of Antwerp. If they could take the city quickly, they might be able to swing south and capture the rest of the Channel ports. In October the king of Belgium and what remained of his army retreated to the heavily fortified Antwerp. The British decided to send a high-ranking representative to try to convince the king not to surrender. Churchill, eager as ever for action, volunteered.

He arrived in Antwerp along with eight thousand troops and took complete charge of the defense of the city. He gave orders to Belgian generals, and even to the king, as if they were private soldiers. As usual, he threw himself wholeheartedly into the venture, going so far as to telegraph Asquith

The Germans take the offensive at the start of World War I. Knowing they were at a disadvantage at sea, the Germans planned to attack France on land.

offering to resign as First Lord in exchange for appointment as a general.

After the cabinet had had a good laugh, Asquith refused the offer. He wired Churchill that a general currently in Dunkerque, France, just west of the Belgian border, would be sent as commander at Antwerp. Until the general arrived, however, Churchill was in charge. An Italian journalist recorded this picture of Churchill in Antwerp:

> He was still young and was enveloped in a cloak, and on his head wore a yachtsman's cap. He was tranquilly smoking a large cigar and looking at the progress of the battle under a rain of shrapnel [shell fragments], which I can only call fearful. It was Mr. Churchill, who had come to view the situation himself. It must be confessed that it is not easy to find in the whole of Europe a Minister who would be capable of smoking peacefully under that shellfire. He smiled and looked quite satisfied.[70]

At length, the British general arrived, but with no new troops. Churchill decided that the city, heavily shelled by the Germans, could not resist any longer. The Belgians surrendered and the British retreated. More than fifteen hundred British marines had been killed and two battalions were captured. Because of the loss of British troops, and of Antwerp itself, the entire episode was called a failure, especially by Conservatives, who blamed Churchill. "What about Antwerp?" was now part of the anti-Churchill vocabulary, along with "What about Tonypandy?"

But was it such a failure? The defense of Antwerp had held up the Germans for

---

A Fresh Wind at the Admiralty

The British navy had grown complacent with no one to challenge it. When Germany began to emerge as a threat before World War I, Churchill, as First Lord of the Admiralty, brought a new vigor to the navy, as Violet Bonham Carter relates in Churchill: An Intimate Portrait.

"The impact of [Churchill's] personality vibrated through the Admiralty. He decreed that naval officers as well as resident clerks should be on duty night and day on weekdays, Sundays and holidays, so that in the event of a surprise attack no moment should be lost in giving the alarm. He also ordered a large chart of the North Sea to be hung up on the wall behind his chair. On this chart a staff officer marked the position of the German Fleet with flags. 'I made it a rule to look at my chart once every day when I first entered the room. I did this less to keep myself informed . . . than in order to inculcate [instill] in myself and those working with me a sense of ever-present danger. In this spirit we all worked.' Instancy was his watchword."

Churchill originated the idea of the tank, first used in World War I. During World War I tanks proved valuable in making progress beyond the trenches.

seven days. Without this delay, the Germans might have taken the Channel ports. The British *Official History of the War* said the defense of Antwerp "had a lasting influence on the operations. Until Antwerp had fallen the [Germans] were not available to move forward and . . . were too late to turn the northern flank of the Allies as intended."[71]

War in the Trenches

The war quickly became a standoff. The armies faced each other from trenches reaching from the English Channel more than six hundred miles to the Swiss border. Between the trenches was "no-man's-land," blasted by shellfire and covered with rolls of barbed wire. Every so often, one side or the other would attack. A hundred yards of ground might be captured at a cost of thousands of lives.

A new idea was needed. Churchill suggested a metal shield "pushed along either on a wheel or still better on a Caterpillar [a type of tractor]."[72] By early 1915, he had improved his idea to "a number of steam tractors with small armoured shelters, in which men and machine guns would be bullet-proof."[73] He ordered a "land ship" designed. To keep the project secret, those working on it said they were making water tanks for Russia. The name stuck, and Churchill's new weapon would evermore be known as the tank. In 1918 tank divisions would make the first serious break in the German line.

An Imaginative Plan

In the meantime, however, something else was needed to break the deadlock of trench warfare. In November 1914, Churchill first proposed an attack on the Dardanelles, the thin body of water in Turkey connecting the Aegean Sea and the Sea of Marmara. If the Dardanelles could be taken, a British fleet could force the surrender of the Turkish capital of Constantinople on the eastern coast of the Sea of Marmara. This would knock Turkey out of the war, provide a route to supply Russia, and open the way for an attack on Austria and Germany from the southeast.

Military historian Alan Moorehead wrote that the Dardanelles plan was "the most imaginative conception of the war, and its potentialities were almost beyond reckoning."[74] Another writer said that had the plan worked, "not only the entire development of the First World War but also the fate of Britain, and Europe, too, would have been different."[75] The war might have been shortened by years, and a well-supplied Russia might not have been the victim of the Bolshevik revolution in 1917.

The plan, however, failed—thanks to incredible bungling on the part of the British. Churchill first thought the campaign could succeed only if the navy were aided by army troops, who would seize from the Turks the Gallipoli peninsula on the north side of the

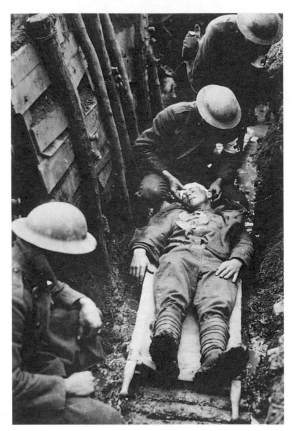

World War I was mostly fought in trenches, ditches that stretched for miles. These defensive trenches left troops virtually immobile since to go out into the open to attack meant being mowed down by the enemy.

Dardanelles. The head of the War Office was none other than Lord Kitchener, Churchill's old acquaintance from the Sudan. Kitchener said that no troops could be spared from France.

The British admiral in the eastern Mediterranean, however, said the Dardanelles could be forced by the navy alone—that the ships' guns and small landing parties of marines could silence the Turkish forts on Gallipoli. Churchill enthusiastically presented the plan to the cabinet, which was just as enthusiastic.

Failure in the Dardanelles

The attack began on February 19, 1915, with British ships raining shells on the Turkish forts. The bombardment continued into March. The Turks, almost out of ammunition, were ready to surrender. Then, on March 18, British ships advancing into the channel sailed too close to shore; they ran into a minefield, and three battleships were sunk. Instead of continuing, the admiral lost his nerve, called off the assault, and told London that army troops, after all, would be needed to take Gallipoli.

Churchill telegraphed the admiral, urging him to renew the attack. The admiral wouldn't budge. Kitchener finally decided that British troops could be spared from France, but he delayed an entire month before sending them to the Mediterranean. In the meantime, the Turks rushed men and ammunition to Gallipoli. By the time the British troops landed in late April, they faced fierce resistance and suffered heavy loss of life.

Turkish and British troops face off in Gallipoli. Due to bureaucratic and military bungling, the British suffered fierce resistance and heavy loss of life in the campaign.

Initially, the British navy was successful in the Gallipoli campaign. Here, HMS Cornwallis *fires on the Turks.*

The British public looked for someone to blame. That someone was Churchill. The Conservatives, still furious at Churchill for switching parties, made him their prime target. The Conservative leader, Andrew Bonar Law, demanded that Asquith form a coalition government—one in which the cabinet would be made up of both Conservatives and Liberals. Bonar Law had one condition: Churchill must be dismissed. Asquith agreed.

Churchill was crushed. He had been so deeply involved in military matters that he had no idea of the political forces mounting against him. Soon after he was dismissed, Churchill saw Violet Asquith, who wrote that he was "silent, despairing—as I had never seen him. He seemed to have no rebelliousness or even anger left. He . . . simply said, 'I'm finished.'"[76]

Churchill fell into deep despair. "I thought he would die of grief," said Clementine.[77] Throughout his life, Churchill suffered from periods of depression. He had even had a name for them—his "Black Dog." On this occasion, he was pulled from his dark mood when he took up painting as a hobby. His secretary said the painting "was a distraction and a sedative that brought a measure of ease to his frustrated spirit."[78] He would find comfort in painting the rest of his life, and even exhibited at the Royal Academy of Art under the name "Charles Morin."

Asquith, to spare Churchill's feelings, offered to keep him in the cabinet in the position of chancellor of the Duchy of Lancaster, an outdated and mostly ceremonial job. He accepted, but stayed only until November. He had no influence and had become merely a spectator to great events. He decided he would rather fight in France.

A Soldier Once Again

The British commander in France offered to make Churchill a brigadier general, but Asquith, fearing the reaction of the Conservatives, would not allow it. Instead, Churchill, who had some years before obtained a commission in the Queen's Own Oxfordshire Hussars (mostly for exercise), joined the regiment in France as a major near the end of 1915. His reception was not warm. His battalion commander told him frostily, "I think I ought to tell you we were not at all consulted about your coming to us."[79]

Conditions in the trenches must have been a shock to Churchill, used to a life of luxury. But he made the best of it. Amid all the mud, filth, death, and decay, he wrote Clementine, "I have found happiness & content such as I have not known for many months."[80] He became popular with the troops. He was promoted to the next rank, lieutenant colonel, and put in command of a battalion.

Yet, Churchill was wasting his time, and he knew it. His abilities were needed more in government than in the trenches. He returned to England on May 7, 1916, to take his seat as an ordinary member of Parliament. He spent most of the next few months defending himself before an investigation of the Dardanelles campaign, which had ended with 213,980 British killed

Britain Goes to War

In 1914 Great Britain issued an ultimatum: If Germany did not remove troops from neutral Belgium, a state of war would exist between the two countries. The deadline for replying to the ultimatum was 11 P.M. on August 4, 1914. In Volume I of The World Crisis, *Churchill described the dawning of war.*

"The minutes passed slowly. Once more now in the march of centuries Old England was to stand forth in battle against the mightiest thrones and dominations. Once more in defence of the liberties of Europe and the common right must she enter upon a voyage of great toil and hazard across waters uncharted, towards coasts unknown, guided only by the stars. Once more 'the far-off line of storm-beaten ships' was to stand between the Continental Tyrant and the dominion of the world. It was 11 o'clock at night . . . when the ultimatum expired. . . . Along the Mall [a London street] from the direction of the Palace the sound of an immense concourse singing 'God Save the King' floated in. On this deep wave there broke the chimes of Big Ben; and, as the first stroke of the hour boomed out, a rustle of movement swept across the room. The war telegram, which meant 'Commence hostilities against Germany' was flashed to the ships and establishments under the White Ensign all over the world. I walked across the Horse Guards' Parade to the Cabinet room and reported to the Prime Minister and the Ministers who were assembled there that the deed was done."

Father of the Tank

In 1915, Churchill, searching for a way to break the stalemate brought on by trench warfare in Europe, urged that several current ideas be merged to create a new weapon, the tank. In a letter found in Volume I of The World Crisis, *he describes his vision to the prime minister, Herbert Asquith.*

"It would be quite easy in a short time to fit up a number of steam tractors with small armoured shelters, in which men and machine guns could be placed, which would be bullet-proof. Used at night they would not be affected by artillery fire to any extent. The caterpillar system would enable trenches to be crossed quite easily, and the weight of the machine would destroy all wire entanglements. Forty or fifty of these engines prepared secretly and brought into position at nightfall could advance quite certainly into the enemy's trenches with their machine-gun fire and with grenades thrown out of the top. They would then make so many points d'appui [points of support] for the British supporting infantry to rush forward and rally on them. They can then move forward to attack the second line of trenches. The cost would be small. If the experiment did not answer [work], what harm would be done? An obvious measure of prudence would have been to have started something like this two months ago. It should certainly be done now."

Armored tanks, Churchill's idea, helped break the stalemate resulting from trench warfare in World War I.

Churchill speaks to munitions workers in 1918 while serving as munitions minister. Churchill proved a successful minister, increasing weapons production and cutting waste.

and wounded. Although the conclusion of the investigators was that Churchill was not responsible for the failure of the campaign, the public continued to place most of the blame on him.

Late in 1916, Churchill's old friend Lloyd George succeeded Asquith as prime minister. On June 18, 1917, he brought Churchill back into the government, over the violent objections of the Tories, as minister of munitions. Churchill reorganized the department and increased the production of weapons 20 percent. These weapons were used, in part, to supply the Americans, who had entered the war in April.

At last, the Germans were worn down by the Allies' superior numbers and resources. Tanks, increasingly important

A Boy at Heart

Late in World War I, when Churchill was minister of munitions, he and Clementine lived with his sister-in-law, Gwendolyn Churchill, and her son, John Jr. John's account of his famous uncle at play appeared in A Churchill Canvas *and can be found in* Man of the Century *by the Reader's Digest.*

"When my brother, Pebin, and I were given a box of Meccano [a building set] we retreated to the . . . dining room. My uncle drifted in, puffing at the inevitable cigar. 'And what are you making, eh?' he demanded. 'A cantilever crane,' I told him. 'Hm.' The cigar was sucked thoughtfully. 'A bascule bridge would be much better you know.' A secretary was sent out to buy box after box of Meccano. Then, apparently forgetting he had a war on his hands, my uncle took off his coat and began preparing the largest model bascule bridge ever. . . . Protests were made by the womenfolk about the inconvenience of half-finished girders resting across the sideboard, but my uncle refused to be deflected. The final construction was a gigantic piece of engineering some fifteen feet long and eight feet high, with a roadway which could be lifted by means of wheels, pulleys and yards of string. The servants were forbidden to touch it, and my uncle gazed fondly at his creation during meals. Eventually, it proved to be too much of a nuisance in the dining room, stretching as it did from wall to wall across one end, and was transferred into the hall, an even worse site. Visitors, including members of the Cabinet, had to stoop under the raised center section of the bridge to get in and out of the door."

and no longer known as "Winston's folly," played a crucial role. A German general called the tank attack of August 8, 1918, "a black day in the German army."[81] Finally, with his army near revolt, Wilhelm II, the German ruler, fled to neutral Holland. The Germans surrendered on November 11.

World War I was over. Great Britain had sustained more than 3 million casualties: 908,371 killed, 2,090,212 wounded, and 191,652 missing. When the chimes of Big Ben, the clock atop the Houses of Parliament in London, rang out the victory, Churchill felt no joy. As he wrote later, "Victory had been bought so dear [expensively] as to be indistinguishable from defeat."[82]

Chapter

5 Back to the Conservatives

The end of World War I in 1918 was by no means the end of foreign difficulties for Great Britain. Old trouble spots remained, new ones sprang up, and Churchill played important roles in all of them.

The immediate problem was Russia. The Bolshevik Revolution in 1917 had overthrown the Russian monarchy, and the Bolsheviks had signed a peace treaty with the Germans. The Allies were afraid that the end of the war on the eastern border of Germany would allow the Germans to send all their forces to France. The Allies, therefore, sent troops into Russia to fight the Germans, with the idea of keeping Ger-

many occupied on two fronts. They were joined by the "White" (as opposed to the "Red," or Communist) Russians.

After the war, many of the foreign troops stayed in Russia, trying to help the Whites overthrow the Reds and restore the monarchy. No one wanted this more than Churchill, who had been made minister of War and Air (in charge of the army and air force) by Lloyd George. Even though he was concerned about the well-being of the common people, he had a strong sense of class consciousness. He believed the upper classes had a responsibility toward those less powerful, but he

Vladimir Lenin incites the crowds after the Bolshevik Revolution of 1917 that overthrew the Russian monarchy.

was opposed to the sharing of power with the masses. Churchill was an aristocrat both by birth and in outlook. He had a strong sense of order, which required that power be exercised by a select few. To him, a world in which the common people ruled would be a world of chaos.

Thus, naturally, Churchill had an especially violent hatred of communism, which taught that the workers should rise in revolt against the upper classes. In a speech at Dundee in 1918 he called the Bolsheviks "an animal form of barbarism" and added that "the Bolsheviks hop and caper like troops of ferocious baboons amid the ruins of cities and the corpses of their victims."[83] The rest of the world should unite, he said, "to strangle Bolshevism at its birth."[84]

Sympathy for the Communists

Many in the British government shared Churchill's anti-Bolshevik feelings, but no one else spoke as powerfully. At this time, however, many in the working classes saw communism not as a threat from Russia, but as a worldwide movement potentially able to give power to the common people. Much of the British public, therefore, was sympathetic to the Communists and saw in Churchill's support of the White Russians another example of what they believed to be his anti-labor views. It was yet another reason for them to view him as an enemy.

More important, the prime minister, David Lloyd George, was just as unenthusiastic as the British workers about Churchill's goal to restore the Russian monarchy. He complained that Churchill's "ducal blood revolted against the wholesale elimination of the Grand Dukes in Russia."[85] This was the start of a split between Lloyd George and Churchill. The Liberal Party, in fact, was moving closer to the Labour Party and away from Churchill. Despite the help of foreign troops, the White Russians were defeated. By March 1920, all British troops were withdrawn from Russia. The Communists triumphed and began working to establish the Union of Soviet Socialist Republics.

Differences in outlook not withstanding, Lloyd George respected Churchill's abilities. So, in 1921, when Churchill asked for a more important job, he was made head of the colonial office. His first task was to try to bring order to the Middle East. This huge area, including Turkey, Arabia, Palestine, Persia, and Mesopotamia, had been ruled for centuries by the Turks, whose empire had collapsed when the Central Powers were defeated in World War I. At the peace conference in Paris after the war, Britain and France divided Turkey's former possessions between them, with Britain gaining control of Persia, Mesopotamia, and Palestine.

Churchill went to the area in 1922 to try to establish stable governments in each country. He took with him as an advisor Colonel T. E. Lawrence, "Lawrence of Arabia," who had led Arab troops against the Turks during the war and was highly respected in the Middle East. Soon Mesopotamia became the country of Iraq, and Persia became Iran. Churchill made two of the sons of Husein ibn-Ali, Britain's Arab ally during the war, kings over Iraq and Iran. It was agreed that the kings' sons would attend school in England and that Iraq and Iran would look toward Britain for guidance.

Palestine was a much thornier problem. To win the alliance of Jewish settlers in Palestine during World War I, Britain

Aftermath of Intervention

In 1920 Churchill's was the loudest voice in Britain in favor of intervening in Russia to overturn the Communist government. When his policy failed, wrote Robert Rhodes James in Churchill: A Study in Failure, *it reminded everyone of past mistakes.*

"The episode had also demonstrated the fact that the features of Churchill's personality that his critics had found so alarming in the past had not really changed. They considered that in his quests for a policy agreement in the Cabinet he . . . once again, had rushed into a highly complex situation with only a superficial understanding of its difficulties. He had committed very substantial sums of money and much political capital into a venture that aroused his most fierce emotional feelings and which he had not considered in advance with coolness. The episode had brought him little credit either outside or inside the Government, and had effectively revived the apprehensions of 1915 about his judgment and capacity. By his bold public declarations he had identified himself strongly with those who wished to see bolshevism crushed, but by the end he could only claim an efficient withdrawal. His critics could claim with some justice that their forecasts had been abundantly justified. The episode opened a schism [division] between Churchill and Lloyd George that was never really healed; confirmed Bonar Law in his hostile view of Churchill's reliability and common sense; and alienated Labour yet again."

had come out in favor of an independent Jewish nation in the region. After the war, the Jews called on the British to back up their support with diplomatic action. The Arabs, who made up the vast majority of the population, were violently opposed. In Egypt, mobs threw stones at Churchill's car and shouted threats. Arab leaders hinted that they might seek an alliance with Russia or even Germany if Britain pursued the possibility of a Jewish state.

Doing the "Honest Thing"

Churchill, not one to be bullied, told the Arab leaders that Britain would keep its word. "The position of Great Britain in Palestine is one of trust, but it is also one of right," he said bluntly.[86] "The man's as brave as six," Lawrence wrote to a friend. "Several times I've seen him chuck the statesmanlike course & do the honest thing instead."[87]

Churchill firmly believed in a Jewish homeland. When he returned to England, he told Parliament, "We cannot, after what we have said and done, leave the Jews in Palestine to be mistreated by the Arabs."[88] The speech, wrote one listener, "changed the whole atmosphere of the House on the Middle East question."[89] The House of Commons then passed, 292 to 35, a resolution supporting Churchill.

It would be twenty-five years before the Jewish state, Israel, was created, but Churchill had laid the foundation. He had not brought a lasting peace to the Middle East, but he had achieved a great deal. Historian A.L. Rowse wrote:

> It was . . . a brilliant settlement for which Churchill was responsible. Against all the probabilities—and the Middle East was in an alarming state, out of which it was unlikely any settled order could be wrested—Churchill made a peace settlement that endured up to the Second World War and beyond.[90]

As colonial secretary, Churchill also had to deal with Ireland. Ireland had never truly become—with England, Scotland, and Wales—a part of Great Britain. By the 1800s, Ireland had representatives in Parliament, but its people longed to have their own, independent country. The name of their movement was Sinn Féin ("ourselves alone" in Gaelic).

Ready for a Fight

The question of "home rule" for Ireland had come up again and again in British politics. Ireland, Churchill told Parliament in 1922, had the power to "lay its hands upon the vital strings of British life and politics, and to hold, dominate and convulse, year after year, generation after generation, the politics of this powerful country."[91] During and after the war, the Irish grew tired of trying to get what they wanted through representation in Parliament. They turned toward the Irish Republican Army (IRA), the terrorist arm of Sinn Féin. Bombings and assassinations became common.

Churchill, ready as ever for a fight, first tried to meet force with force. He created a special police force, made up mostly of former British soldiers, to battle the IRA. These police, known as the "Black and Tans" because of the black belts they wore with khaki uniforms, proved as bloodthirsty as the IRA. Their brutality sickened the British public and drove the IRA to more desperate measures.

At first, Churchill approved of the tactics of the Black and Tans. Before long, however, the use of torture by the British became common and it was learned that suspected terrorists were being shot without a trial. Churchill realized that such measures would embitter the Irish so greatly that no peaceful solution would be possible. The Black and Tans were disbanded, and Churchill helped draw up a treaty whereby Ireland would become a "free state" with its own parliament. The head of the government would be a governor-general appointed by the British monarch. This did not satisfy Sinn Féin, who wanted nothing less than a complete break. It also did not please Ulster, the six heavily Protestant counties in northeast Ireland that wanted to stay part of Britain rather than become part of an Irish free state, which would be mostly Roman Catholic.

The Irish Free State

Lloyd George asked Churchill to lead the fight in Parliament to pass the treaty, which was unpopular with the Conservatives. Churchill told the House of Commons it was "high time that the main body of Irish and British opinion asserted its determination to put a stop to these fanatical quarrels."[92] Parliament approved the treaty on December 23, 1921. The southern twenty-six counties of Ireland would become the Irish Free State. Ulster would remain part of Britain.

Now Ireland had to be persuaded to accept the treaty. Two representatives of Sinn Féin, Arthur Griffith and Michael Collins, came to London for talks. Churchill was the chief negotiator for Britain. At one point during a private meeting, Collins grew angry and said, "You hunted me day and night. You put a price on my head." Churchill took down

Churchill at Home

Churchill loved Chartwell, his country home in Kent, and spent as much time there as possible. This account of his home life in the 1920s, from Winston Churchill: The Era and the Man, *is found in* Man of the Century, *compiled by the* Reader's Digest.

"Winston seldom spent a weekend away from his country house. Chartwell was close enough to London for lunch and dinner, and almost every Saturday and Sunday there were relays of people coming and going. Winston's favorite relaxation was good political talk. He liked to sit up late at night, woke early in the morning, often did his work in bed, dictating to his secretary and puffing a cigar. His morning work was interrupted frequently by the shouts and cries of his four children, who ranged in age from eleven to one; and when the din was too great he put aside his work and joined them in the garden. They adored his company. He put up a tree house, showed them how to dam the lake and make miniature falls. Like the children themselves, he got so wet he stood dripping outside the house while maids hurried to put newspapers on the floor. He had never forgotten how he himself had longed for his father's confidence and he spent many hours with his son, talking to him as a grown-up and letting him share his interests. Once when he drove Randolph back to Eton he remarked sadly: 'I have talked to you more this holiday than my father talked to me in his whole life.'"

from his wall a reward poster issued after his escape from the Boers. "At any rate," he told Collins, "it was a good price—5,000 pounds. Look at me—25 pounds dead or alive. How would you like that?"[93] The two men laughed and became friends, and the Irish visitors accepted the treaty. Churchill had put southern Ireland on the path that would lead it to independence as the nation of Eire in 1937.

Foreign affairs took a backseat to politics for Churchill in 1922. When the Conservatives withdrew from the coalition government, Lloyd George resigned and Bonar Law became prime minister. In the general election that November, Churchill was defeated. The working men of Dundee had lost faith in him and had turned to the Labour Party. (Women received the vote in England in 1928.) Many other Liberals lost, as well, and the Conservatives were in power for the first time since 1904.

Churchill had been too ill to do much campaigning. He had his appendix removed and went to Dundee only a few days before the voting. Later, he wrote, "In the twinkling of an eye, I found myself without an office, without a seat [in Parliament], without a party, and without an appendix."[94] At the time, he was far less cheerful. A friend later remembered, "He thought his world would come to an end—at least his political world. I thought his career was over."[95]

To escape from his depression, Churchill began writing *The World Crisis*. The first volume in this six-volume history of World War I appeared in 1923. He threw himself into work on his new country home, Chartwell, bought with an inheritance from a great grandmother. He painted for hours.

Churchill painted this still life during the years after the 1904 loss of his seat in Parliament. Painting and writing were his consolation during this depressing period.

After he lost his seat in Parliament, Churchill purchased Chartwell with an inheritance from his great grandmother. Work on his new country home helped him to keep busy.

Another Chance, Another Defeat

Another political opportunity arose in 1923. Bonar Law had resigned because of poor health. Stanley Baldwin, a rich industrialist who had climbed in a slow and unspectacular fashion through the Conservative Party ranks, became prime minister and called an election. Churchill ran as a Liberal in West Leicester and was defeated again. Once more, his past followed him as crowds shouted, "What about Tonypandy?" "What about Antwerp?" "What about the Dardanelles?"

No party had won a clear majority, and the Liberals teamed up with Labour to form a government, headed by Ramsay MacDonald, Britain's first Labour prime minister. Churchill hated the Labour Party as much as its members hated him. As far back as 1908 he had drawn the line between liberalism and socialism. "Socialism seeks to pull down wealth," he said. "Liberalism seeks to raise up poverty."[96]

Churchill began to move back to the Conservatives. In 1924 he ran as an independent candidate in the Westminster Abbey district of London. Despite hard work by his backers, who ranged from the duke of Marlborough to chorus girls from Daly Theatre, and the private support of Stanley Baldwin, he lost by forty-two votes.

This time, however, he was not discouraged. He had made up his mind to return

Churchill and his wife in Epping during his campaign to regain a seat in Parliament. He won the seat easily and would continue to represent Epping throughout his career.

to the Conservatives. The union between the Liberals and Labour lasted only a few months, and another election was held. Churchill, now a Tory once again, ran in Epping (about thirty miles north of London) and won easily. He would represent Epping for the rest of his long parliamentary career.

The Conservatives won, as well. Baldwin, prime minister once more, wanted Churchill in his cabinet. In addition to respecting Churchill's ability, he was afraid that Churchill, if left out, might join with Lloyd George to revive the Liberals. Baldwin sent for Churchill and asked if he would serve as chancellor. "Of the Duchy?" asked Churchill, remembering his dismissal from the Admiralty in 1915. "No," said Baldwin, "of the Exchequer."[97]

Many Conservatives protested the appointment. How, they asked Baldwin, could he make someone who only a few months ago was a member of another party the second most powerful man in the government? Baldwin's answer was simple: "Winston is the ablest mind in politics."[98]

Churchill was not, however, the right man to head Britain's treasury. One economist, Hubert Henderson, wrote that he was "one of the worst Chancellors of the Exchequer of modern times."[99] He was, at least, better than his father, Lord Randolph, who could never figure out what the decimal points in the national budget meant, calling them "those damned dots."[100]

Churchill's experience had prepared him for his offices in the Admiralty and colonial affairs. He understood military and colonial matters, but not economics or finance. He complained that "If [economists] were soldiers or generals I would understand what they were talking about. As it is, they all talk Persian."[101]

Guided mainly by his own instincts, which were not well informed, Churchill made mistakes. The most serious error was to return Britain in 1925 to the gold standard. This meant that the British pound decreased in value and prices went up. In addition, British exports became more expensive for other countries. At home, workers' wages would buy less.

The General Strike

The industry most affected by the devaluation accompanying the return to the gold standard was coal, Britain's chief export. British coal became more expensive overseas, and business declined. Many coal miners lost their jobs, and those still working could not buy as much with their wages. The miners walked out of the pits in 1926 and were soon joined by all the other labor unions in a general strike.

Churchill saw the general strike as an attempt to force the government to bow to workers' demands. At Baldwin's suggestion, he became editor of the *British Gazette*, a newspaper run by the government. Since all other newspapers had been shut down by the strike, the British public got its information only from the *British Gazette*, which presented only the government's side. Public opinion went against the unions, and the strike failed. The government had won, but Churchill had again earned the hatred of the working class.

Economic conditions continued to worsen. In the general election of 1929, voters turned their backs on the Conservatives, and MacDonald again became prime minister. Churchill had been reelected and now was among the leaders of the opposition—but not for long.

The India Question

In 1930 Churchill split with the Conservative Party on the question of making India, then a British colony, a dominion. Churchill saw the proposed move as a step to the breakup of the British Empire. This excerpt from a speech in Parliament is found in Robert Rhodes James's Churchill: A Study in Failure.

"There is a sombre [gloomy] philosophy nowadays which I hear in some quarters about Egypt and India. It is said : 'Give them all they ask for! Clear out and let things go to smash, and then there will be a case for us to come back again.' The action of His Majesty's government would bear that construction. . . . Such a doctrine is no foundation for the continuance of British fame and power. Once we lose confidence in our mission in the East, once we repudiate our responsibilities to foreigners and to minorities, once we feel ourselves unable calmly and fearlessly to discharge our duties to vast helpless populations, then our presence in these countries will be stripped of every moral sanction, and, resting only upon selfish interests or military requirements, it will be a presence which cannot long endure."

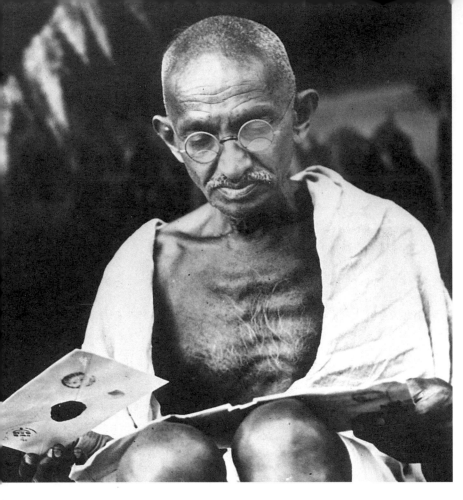

Mohandas Gandhi was an outspoken supporter of Indian self-rule. Churchill was vehemently opposed to allowing India to break from British rule.

India was clamoring for independence, led by a London-trained lawyer named Mohandas Gandhi. Churchill was completely opposed. He was, in many ways, what would later be called a racist. Self-rule, he thought, was fine for white people in South Africa, Ireland, or Australia, but not for Indians. He called Gandhi a "fakir [mystic] of a type well known in the East, striding half-naked up the steps of the Vice-Regal Palace to parley on equal terms with the representative of the King-Emperor."[102]

When the Conservatives supported the Labour government in making India a dominion (self-governing) instead of a colony,

Churchill spoke strongly against it, angering his Tory colleagues. Finally, in January 1931, he resigned from the party leadership. He now was powerless, hated by the party in power and rejected by his own.

Churchill had lost his influence just when Britain needed it most. A new political party had arisen in Germany, the Nationalsozialistische Deutsche Arbeitpartei (National Socialist Workers Party)—Nazi, for short. Its leader was a former Austrian corporal named Adolf Hitler. Churchill's would be one of the only voices raised against him, but, in the 1930s, no one listened.

Chapter

6 The Wilderness

In early 1931, Churchill was fifty-six years old, out of office, out of influence with his own party, and out of favor with much of the British public. Many thought his political life over. Yet, he could not retire. He saw Nazi Germany's threat to England and considered it his duty to speak out, even if he was alone.

The Treaty of Versailles, signed at the end of World War I, had treated Germany harshly. Churchill was one of the few British leaders who thought the victors should have been more lenient. He had argued that harsh treatment of the Germans would only create a desire for revenge. As early as 1925, he had written:

The signing of the Treaty of Versailles, which officially ended World War I. Churchill disagreed with the treaty, saying it would lead the Germans to seek revenge. The harshness of the treaty's terms would indeed lead directly to World War II.

From one end of Germany to the other an intense hatred of France unites the whole population. The enormous contingents of German youth growing to military manhood year by year are inspired by the fiercest sentiments, and the soul of Germany smoulders with dreams of a War of Liberation or Revenge.[103]

No one in Germany wanted revenge more than Adolf Hitler. He was bitter at the country's leaders for having made what he thought was a shameful peace. He also blamed the Jews for the ruin of Germany. In 1919, after attending a meeting of the then-tiny Nazi Party, he had become its seventh member, and soon its leader. By 1923 there were forty-nine thousand members, including some prominent Germans.

The worldwide economic depression spread to Germany in 1930, throwing thousands out of work, and many of the newly unemployed turned to Hitler. In the national election of 1930, the Nazis became the second largest party in the Reichstag, the German legislature.

Not Fooled by Hitler

The Nazis were known for brutal tactics, such as the beating of opponents and the smashing of shops owned by Jews, but Hitler told the world he wanted only peace and many people believed him. Lloyd George wrote that Hitler was the "greatest living German" and "a born leader" who would "never invade another land."[104] The foreign secretary, Sir John Simon, called Hitler "rather retiring and bashful" and "unconcerned with affairs in Western Europe."[105] Churchill was not fooled. A German diplomat reported in

Nazis march in procession prior to World War II. Adolf Hitler was able to gather support by stirring up the Germans' feelings of anger and discontent.

1930 that despite Hitler's promises of peace, Churchill "is convinced that Hitler or his followers will seize the first available opportunity to resort to armed force."[106]

Actually, others perceived the danger of Hitler and his Nazis but chose to do nothing. The leaders of Britain at this time were not men of action. The Labour Party's Ramsay MacDonald, prime minister from 1931 to 1934, hated war and wanted nothing to do with another one. Churchill once called him the "boneless wonder" because of his inaction.[107] He thought little more of the Conservatives' Stanley Baldwin, of whom he once said, "Occasionally he stumbled over the truth, but hastily picked himself up and hurried on as if nothing happened."[108]

These men, however, reflected the country as a whole. Britain was tired of war and wanted only peace. Many of the country's leaders, moreover, saw Hitler and a strong Germany as a barrier to something they feared more—the Soviet Union and the spread of communism. According to historian T.R. Fehrenbach, "The Conservative Government . . . was too intent upon the threatened social revolution to see the imminent nationalist revolt Hitler's Germany was mounting against the democratic world."[109]

Disarmament

Incredibly, one way in which the British—and other European countries—sought to prevent war was by making themselves militarily weak. They thought the international race to build up armed forces had caused World War I. Therefore, if nations disarmed, there would be no war. Churchill thought this was ridiculous. In 1932 he

Ramsay MacDonald, British prime minister from 1931 to 1934, saw the danger in Hitler's rise to power but refused to do anything about it, reluctant to involve Britain in another war.

asked those who argued for disarmament in Parliament, "Do you wish for War?"[110]

Disarmament, however, would be effective only if all nations were committed to it. Germany, Churchill had discovered, had no intention of disarming. Hitler had become president in 1933 and Germany soon was filled with "flying clubs," most of whose members were young men learning to be military pilots, and "sports clubs," whose outdoor activities resembled army maneuvers. German factories began to build airplanes and submarines, in violation of the Treaty of Versailles.

This did not seem to faze Britain's leaders, but it did alarm many younger officers

Warning Against Germany

On November 2, 1932, Churchill gave his first major warning on Germany in the House of Commons. This excerpt from the speech, found in Robert Rhodes James's Churchill: A Study in Failure, *is an answer to those who favored allowing Germany to rearm.*

"Now the demand is that Germany should be allowed to rearm. Do not delude yourselves. Do not let His Majesty's Government believe, I am sure they do not believe, that all that Germany is asking for is equal status. . . .That is not what Germany is seeking. All these bands of sturdy Teutonic youths, marching through the streets and roads of Germany, with the light of desire in their eyes to suffer for their Fatherland, are not looking for status. They are looking for weapons, and, when they have the weapons, believe me they will then ask for the return of their lost territories and lost colonies. . . . Compare the state of Europe on the morrow of [day after] Locarno [a peace treaty in 1924] with its condition today. Fears are greater, rivalries are sharper, military plans are more closely concerted, military organisations are more carefully and efficiently developed, Britain is weaker; and Britain's hour of weakness is Europe's hour of danger."

and government workers. These men, whose careers would have ended had they been discovered, began slipping information to Churchill on the speed of German rearmament. Churchill, who also had sources of information in Europe, soon was the best-informed person in Britain on what was happening in Germany.

A Fearful Warning

In 1934 Churchill gave what would be the first of many speeches on air defense in the House of Commons. He warned his colleagues that

the crash of bombs exploding in London and cataracts of masonry and fire and smoke will apprise us of an inadequacy which has been permitted in our aerial defences. We are as vulnerable as we have never been before. . . . I cannot conceive how, in the present state of Europe and our position in Europe, we can delay in establishing the principle of having our Air Force at least as strong as that of any power that can get at us.[111]

Later that year, in yet another speech, he left no doubt who he thought that power would be. "Germany already, at this moment, has a military air force . . . which only awaits an order to assemble in full open combination," he said. "And this illegal air force is rapidly approaching equality with our own."[112]

He was speaking, however, to a mostly empty House of Commons. Except for a handful of supporters, the few members who stayed when he got up to speak either read or dozed in their seats. Neither was the country paying attention. It couldn't. Most of the leading newspapers, especially the *Times* (London), ignored his speeches, and the British Broadcasting Corporation (BBC) refused his requests to speak on radio.

Baldwin, now prime minister in a Conservative-Labour coalition government, dismissed Churchill's concerns. He pledged that the government was "determined in no condition to accept any position of inferiority with regard to whatever air force might be raised by Germany in the future."[113] During the general election of 1935, he told voters they had nothing to fear. The voters believed him and gave the Conservatives a solid majority.

Both Baldwin and the country then were shocked when, on March 7, 1936, Hitler's troops marched into the Rhineland, a strip of land on the east bank of the Rhine River in Germany that was supposed to remain demilitarized. It was a clear violation of the Treaty of Versailles. Hitler had gambled that the feeble governments of the democracies would not move against him. He proved to be correct.

Even Baldwin now realized something would have to be done. He agreed to name a minister for Coordination of Defence. Public opinion was beginning to turn, and many thought the post should go to Churchill. But Baldwin said, "If I pick Winston, Hitler will be cross."[114] Instead, he chose Sir Thomas Inskip, an attorney with no military experience at all.

Churchill continued to hammer away. On November 12, 1936, he gave his most stinging charge against Britain's leaders:

The Government simply cannot make up their minds, or they cannot get the Prime Minister to make up his mind. So they go on in strange paradox, decided only to be undecided, resolved to be irresolute, adamant for drift, solid for fluidity, all-powerful to be impotent. So we go on preparing more months and years—precious, perhaps vital to the greatest of Britain—for the locusts to eat.[115]

A Startling Admission

In the British system of government, the prime minister responds directly to criticisms from members of Parliament. In his reply to Churchill in the House of Commons, Baldwin said, "Supposing I had gone to the country, and said that Germany was rearming and that we must rearm. . . . I cannot think of anything that would have made the loss of the election from my point of view more certain."[116] Baldwin's admission that he had put party politics before the country's defense shocked Parliament. Churchill appeared to be gaining his colleagues' respect. Then he threw it all away.

The king of Great Britain, Edward VIII, was at age forty-two, still unmarried. However, he had fallen in love with an American woman, Mrs. Wallis Simpson, who was going through a second divorce. Edward, as king, was the titular head of the Church of England, which disapproves of divorce. It seemed that if the king were to marry Mrs. Simpson, he would have to abdicate—give up his throne.

Churchill became Edward's chief defender, a most unpopular position. Baldwin, most of Parliament, and most of the British public were convinced that Edward was obliged to abdicate. When Churchill spoke up for the king in the House of Commons, he was shouted down by the members, one of whom later wrote that Churchill "had undone in five minutes the patient reconstruction work of two years."[117] Edward gave up his throne on December 16. Churchill wrote Edward's radio address to the people.

In May 1937 Baldwin announced his retirement. The new prime minister was Neville Chamberlain, the former chancellor of the exchequer. Although he came from a political family (his father, former chancellor of the exchequer Joe Chamberlain, had aided Churchill in his first successful election), Neville was a businessman and brought that approach to government. He was more interested in a balanced budget than in the balance of military power. He was not, like Baldwin, indecisive. Rather, wrote future prime minister Harold Macmillan, he was "only too sure that he was right on every question. . . . The only trouble with that was that when he was wrong, he was terribly wrong."[118]

He was certainly wrong about Adolf Hitler. Chamberlain considered himself a reasonable man and thought Hitler would listen to reason. Chamberlain was a man of his word and thought Hitler would keep his. He was dreadfully mistaken on both counts. Hitler was demanding *lebensraum* ("living space") for the German people and would do anything to get it.

Hitler's first target was Austria, where the Nazis had become powerful. Early in 1938, he demanded that a leading Nazi be brought into the Austrian cabinet. Austria

Prime Minister Neville Chamberlain refused to believe that Adolf Hitler had plans to invade Europe. In order to avoid war, Chamberlain offered no reprisal to Hitler's initial invasion of Austria.

refused and appealed for help. Britain and France said that, while they were sympathetic, there was nothing they could do. German troops crossed the border on March 11, and Austria became part of Germany.

Proposal for an Alliance

Churchill, alarmed, proposed that Britain form an alliance with Czechoslovakia, Yugoslavia, and Romania, the nations he feared would be Hitler's next targets. Their combined strength, he said, would be enough to resist Germany. When Chamberlain called the concept ridiculous, Churchill asked the House, "What is there ridiculous about collective security? The only thing that is ridiculous is that we haven't got it."[119]

The government wouldn't hear of such an alliance, however. Since disarmament hadn't worked, it was following a new policy called "appeasement." That is, to avoid war, Britain and other countries would give in to Hitler's demands. It was hoped that these concessions would satisfy the Nazi leader.

Germany and Austria combined now surrounded the northern part of Czechoslovakia, known as the Sudetenland and populated mainly by the people of German origin. Hitler had assured the rest of the world that after Austria, he wanted no more territory. Now, he claimed the Sude-

tenland as part of Germany and threatened to take it by force.

Chamberlain was determined to avoid war. He flew to Hitler's mountain retreat of Berchtesgaden and offered a plan whereby the Sudetenland would become German if the people voted to approve the change. Hitler first agreed, but changed his mind two weeks later. Chamberlain then met Hitler again and said that Britain would stand aside and not object if the Sudetenland and all the Czech war matériel there, including fortresses and stores of food and supplies, were to go to Germany without a vote, if Hitler would demand no more territory.

The Czechs refused to turn over their country, and war appeared unavoidable. The Czechs mobilized their army, and

In what would later be seen as a terrible mistake in judgment, Chamberlain, in order to avoid war, continued to allow Hitler to seize land. (Left) Chamberlain leaves for Germany in an attempt to reach an agreement with Hitler. (Right) Chamberlain meets with Hitler.

After agreeing to all of Hitler's demands, and thus avoiding war, Chamberlain returns home to a hero's welcome, waving the so-called no war document. His and other European leaders' attempts to appease Hitler turned out to be in the worst possible judgment.

France, which had a treaty with Czechoslovakia, mobilized along the Maginot line, a series of forts along the border between France and Germany, built after World War I to prevent another invasion from the east.

Chamberlain went to Germany again on September 29, 1938, this time to the city of Munich. He, along with representatives of France and Italy, agreed to all of Hitler's demands. The Czechs did not even participate in the talks. Chamberlain flew back to London to a hero's welcome. War had been avoided. To cheering crowds outside Number 10 Downing Street, he said the Munich agreement meant "peace in our time." [120]

Many Britons were not so sure. Churchill had been at a dinner that included several cabinet ministers when the newspapers came out with details of the agreement. When these were read, there was silence. "Nobody attempted to defend them," wrote one observer. "Humiliation took almost material shape." [121] Alfred Duff Cooper, a friend of Churchill but a loyal member of Chamberlain's cabinet, left the room without a word. He soon resigned.

Britain's "Bitter Cup"

Churchill certainly was not without words. In Parliament, he said, "We have suffered a total and unmitigated defeat." Then he continued:

And do not suppose that this is the end. This is only the beginning of the reckoning. This is only the first sip, the first foretaste of a bitter cup which will be proffered to us year by year unless by a supreme recovery of moral health and martial vigour, we arise again and take our stand for freedom as in the olden time.[122]

When a vote on the Munich agreement was taken, thirty Conservative members abstained—a slap at Chamberlain's government. Even Clement Attlee, the Labour Party leader, described Munich as "a victory for brute force."[123] The tide was finally turning in Churchill's favor.

Churchill, Hitler Almost Meet

The two great antagonists of World War II, Winston Churchill and Adolf Hitler, never encountered each other personally, but they almost met during the summer of 1932 when Churchill was on a visit to Munich, Germany. He described the occasion in The Gathering Storm.

"At the Regina Hotel a gentleman introduced himself to some of my party. He was Herr [Ernst] Hanfstaengl, and spoke a great deal about 'the Fuehrer' [German for 'leader,' as Hitler was known], with whom he appeared to be intimate. . . . He said I ought to meet him, and that nothing would be easier to arrange. Herr Hitler came every day to the hotel about five o'clock, and would be very glad to see me. I had no national prejudices against Hitler at this time. I knew little of his doctrine or record and nothing of his character. I admire men who stand up for their country in defeat, even though I am on the other side. . . . However, in the course of conversation with Hanfstaengl, I happened to say, 'Why is your chief so violent about the Jews? I can quite understand being angry with Jews who have done wrong or against the country . . . but what is the sense of being against a man simply because of his birth?' . . . He must have repeated this to Hitler, because about noon the next day he came round with rather a serious air and said that the appointment he had made with me to meet Hitler could not take place, as the Fuehrer would not be coming to the hotel that afternoon. . . . Thus Hitler lost his only chance of meeting me. Later on, when he was all-powerful, I was to receive several invitations from him. But by that time a lot had happened, and I excused myself."

Hitler had assured Chamberlain that he wanted only the Sudetenland, not the rest of Czechoslovakia. But in March 1939 he broke yet another promise. German troops crossed the border into what remained of Czechoslovakia. On March 15, Hitler entered the Czech capital of Prague in triumph, at the head of his army.

Now, even Chamberlain was alarmed. The next logical target for Hitler was Poland, immediately to the east of Germany, and north of Czechoslovakia. The Soviet Union, Poland's neighbor on the other side, was also becoming nervous and contacted Britain about a possible alliance. When Chamberlain delayed, however, the Soviet leader, Joseph Stalin, began to negotiate with Hitler. Stalin did not trust Britain: He had seen first Austria, then Czechoslovakia, abandoned.

World War II Begins

On August 23, 1939, Germany and the Soviet Union signed a nonaggression pact.

Members of Parliament were not as supportive of Chamberlain's concessions to Hitler as the British public appeared to be. Churchill was especially dismayed, as can be seen in this photo, taken after a conference with Chamberlain.

The Lesson of Munich

In The Gathering Storm, *written after World War II, Churchill ended his account of the Munich conference, at which France and Britain abandoned Czechoslovakia, with this discussion of the use of force.*

"Those who are prone by temperament and character to seek sharp and clear-cut solutions of difficult and obscure problems, who are ready to fight whenever some challenge comes from a foreign Power, have not always been right. On the other hand, those whose inclination is to bow their heads, to seek patiently and faithfully for peaceful compromise, are not always wrong. . . . How many wars have been averted by patience and persisting good will! . . . How many wars have been precipitated [started] by firebrands! . . . The Sermon on the Mount is the last word in Christian ethics. . . . Still, it is not on these terms that Ministers assume their responsibilities of guiding states. Their duty is first so to deal with other nations as to avoid strife and war and to eschew [avoid] aggression in all its forms, whether for nationalistic or ideological objects. But the safety of the State, the lives and freedom of their own fellow countrymen, to whom they owe their position, make it right and imperative in the last resort, or when a final and definite conviction has been reached, that the use of force should not be excluded. If the circumstances are such as to warrant it, force may be used. And if this be so, it should be used under the conditions which are most favourable. There is no merit in putting off a war for a year if, when it comes, it is a far worse war or one much harder to win."

Hitler immediately began to make demands on Poland, but Chamberlain, to his credit, did not repeat the mistake of Munich. On August 25, an alliance between Britain and Poland was announced.

Hitler would not back down. He was determined to attack Poland and was confident that Britain and France, once more, would do nothing. At dawn on September 1, German tanks rolled across the Polish border. At first, Chamberlain again tried to avoid war. He demanded that Germany withdraw. Hitler ignored him. Finally, on September 3, Great Britain declared war on

Hitler had no intention of honoring his agreement to stop his aggression with the invasion of the Sudetenland. Soon his troops were moving into Poland (left). Because of his prediction that such a move would follow the Munich agreement, Churchill (right) gained credibility and was returned to his position of First Lord of the Admiralty.

Germany. France followed one day later.

The press, the public, and Parliament demanded that Churchill be made part of the cabinet. Chamberlain had no choice. Churchill, the voice in the wilderness, had been right all along. To his delight, Chamberlain gave him his old job—First Lord of the Admiralty. A signal went out to every ship in the Royal Navy—"Winston is back."[124]

Chapter

7 His Finest Hour

For years Winston Churchill had warned Britain about Hitler and Nazi Germany. He had mostly been ignored. Now, Britain was once more at war, and for the next five years, during which the survival of democracy hung in the balance, its leader was Churchill.

German bombers pounded cities during the blitzkrieg, *which was almost invincible. Europe could do little to help when Hitler used such tactics to take over Poland.*

Britain and France could do little to help Poland, demolished by a type of warfare the world had never seen. Bombers pounded cities, while waves of tanks swept over Polish soldiers, many of whom charged German tanks on horseback. This was *blitzkrieg* ("lightning war") and Poland lasted only a month.

In the west, British troops took up positions on the northwestern end of the Maginot line. Then, for months, the two sides watched each other. In Britain, this period was known as the "phony war"; in Germany, the *sitzkrieg* ("sitting war").

The only action was in the far north. Sweden and neighboring Norway both were neutral, but Churchill had proposed that Britain take and occupy Norwegian ports, and take over the Swedish iron mines as well, for Sweden was Germany's chief source of iron ore. This would be a clear violation of the neutrality of Sweden and Norway, but Churchill was convinced that unless the British acted, the Germans would occupy both countries. The Chamberlain government debated and delayed, but finally agreed.

Meanwhile, in Britain, it was hard to realize there was a war. Government officials took long weekends. The crisis, it seemed, had passed. Neville Chamberlain, the prime minister, certainly thought so.

In a speech on April 11, 1940, he cheerfully told the country that Hitler had "missed the bus."[125]

Chamberlain did not know that Hitler was moving toward Norway at the same time as the British. The Germans got there first by a few days, taking control of key Norwegian ports. When the British arrived, they landed troops and actually captured the port of Narvik, but were soon forced to withdraw. Sweden would remain neutral throughout the war. Norway, anxious to escape the fate of Poland, submitted to German occupation.

Chamberlain Under Fire

It was obvious that Chamberlain was not an effective wartime prime minister. Churchill, now a loyal member of the cabinet, tried to take the blame for the defeat in Norway before Parliament on May 7. His old friend Lloyd George told him he "must not allow himself to be converted into an air-raid shelter to keep the splinters from hitting his colleagues."[126]

When Chamberlain tried to defend himself, he was attacked from all sides. A fellow Conservative, Leo Amery, shouted, "In the name of God, go!"[127] Chamberlain refused to resign. He tried to form a coalition government, but the Labour Party leaders said they would serve under no one but Churchill.

On the morning of May 10, 1940, the phony war ended. German troops launched an all-out attack on Holland, Belgium, and France. That afternoon, Chamberlain resigned. Churchill was asked by the king to become the new prime minister. He later wrote that he felt "as if I were walking with destiny, and that all my past life had been a preparation for this hour and for this trial."[128]

On May 13, as the Germans smashed through Belgium, Churchill rose in Parliament for the first time as prime minister. He spoke slowly, delivering one of the most famous speeches in history:

> I have nothing to offer but blood, toil, tears, and sweat. . . . You ask, What is our policy? I will say: It is to wage war, by sea, land and air, with all our might and with all the strength that God can give us; to wage war against a monstrous tyranny, never surpassed in the dark, lamentable catalogue of human crime. That is our policy. You ask, what

Germany invaded Belgium, Holland, and France on May 10, 1940. That same day, Chamberlain resigned and Churchill accepted the position of prime minister.

Appreciating the New Boss

When Churchill became prime minister of Britain in 1940, there was some apprehension among those in the government who thought him brilliant but unreliable. One of these was Sir Ian Jacob, a secretary to the War Cabinet, who in Action This Day *told about a change in attitude.*

"Nevertheless, the opinion we formed of Churchill at this time [when he was First Lord of the Admiralty in 1939-40], operating as he was from a subordinate position and yet trying to impart some drive and imagination to the conduct of affairs, was of a tireless and brilliant mind, yet unpredictable and meddlesome, and quite unsuited to handle his colleagues in a team. When we heard he was to be Prime Minister on the fall of Chamberlain I well remember the misgivings of many of us in the War Cabinet Office. We had not the experience or the imagination to realise the difference between a human dynamo when humming on the periphery [outer edge] and when driving at the centre. We were too inclined to respect order and method and to discount initiative and leadership. It wasn't long before we began to see how greatly we had under-rated the quality of the man. Nevertheless, in fairness to our judgment, which wasn't altogether wrong, I must record that in my opinion the lack of administrative understanding displayed by Mr. Churchill would hardly have been counterbalanced by the other qualities he possessed, if he had not been quickly harnessed to a most effective machine, which was ready to his hand without his knowing it."

is our aim? I can answer in one word: victory, victory at all costs, victory in spite of all terror, victory, however long and hard the road may be; for without victory there is no survival.[129]

This speech was the first of many that were to rally and unite the British. It "was a real turning point," wrote Robert Rhodes James. "It stirred the Commons to its depths. It came to the British people as a call to service and sacrifice. It rang round the world."[130] Churchill's speeches in 1940 were to be more important than anything else he accomplished as prime minister. Not only did they unite Britain, they also helped convince the United States and its president, Franklin D. Roosevelt, that the British would somehow win.

At first, however, victory seemed remote. The Germans continued to slice through Holland and Belgium. On May 16, they broke through the Maginot line. The French were disorganized and helpless.

On May 19, Churchill made his first broadcast to the nation as prime minister. He spoke of the nations that had already fallen to Hitler, those "upon whom a long night of barbarism will descend, unbroken by even a star of hope, unless we conquer, as conquer we must, as conquer we shall."[131]

The "Miracle" of Dunkirk

The next day, the German army reached the French city of Abbeville, where the river Somme widens and flows directly into the English Channel. British forces to the north were trapped. They fought their way to the only exit available to them, Dunkerque, some twenty-five miles from the English coast. Churchill ordered all available ships and boats to the little port, now known by its English spelling—Dunkirk. More than 850 civilian and naval vessels of all kinds rescued 338,000 troops.

Dunkirk was hailed as a miracle, but Churchill told Parliament, "Wars are not won by evacuations." He pledged to fight to the last, even if Britain were invaded, saying:

> We shall go on to the end. We shall fight in France, we shall fight on the seas and oceans, we shall fight with growing confidence and growing strength in the air, we shall defend our island, whatever the cost may be. We shall fight on the beaches, we shall fight on the landing grounds, we shall fight in the fields and in the streets, we shall fight in the hills; we shall never surrender.

His next words were directed at the United States, without whose help, he believed, Britain was lost:

> And even if, which I do not for a moment believe, this island or a large part of it were subjugated and starving, then our Empire beyond the seas, armed and guarded by the British fleet, would carry on the struggle, until, in God's good time, the New World, with all its power and might, steps forth to the rescue and liberation of the old.[132]

When British troops were trapped before the advancing Germans on the French coast at Dunkirk, Churchill saved the day by ordering naval ships to evacuate the troops.

Churchill tried everything to convince the French to keep fighting, but they seemed resigned to defeat. Their military leader, Marshal Maxime Weygand, predicted that "In three weeks England would have her neck wrung like a chicken."[133] On June 17, France asked Hitler for peace terms. What Wilhelm's Germany had failed to do in five years of World War I, Hitler had accomplished in six weeks.

The next day, when Churchill told Parliament that the battle of France was over, he continued, "I expect the Battle of Britain is about to begin." Hitler, he continued, "knows that he will have to break us in this island or lose the war. Let us therefore brace ourselves to do our duty and so bear ourselves that if the British Empire and its Commonwealth last for a thousand years men will still say, 'This was their finest hour.'"[134]

One last act remained in the battle of France. To prevent French ships from being used by Hitler, Churchill ordered them seized and, if need be, sunk. At Oran, in French Morocco, the French admirals refused to surrender. Churchill, making "a hateful decision, the most painful in which

All Work, No Play

Churchill's single-minded effort to survive in 1940 occupied every minute of every day. Sir Ian Jacob described the prime minister's work habits in Action This Day.

"In the circumstances of 1940, when the fight for survival was all-absorbing, the whole of his energies were concentrated on this fight, and, although the problem was most complex, there were no distractions. The demands of political life and parliamentary warfare which take up so much time and energy in peacetime were reduced to a minimum. There were no social activities. Except during the hours of sleep every moment could be used for work. Meal-times and journeys by train or car were never wasted, because useful conversations could be held or Minutes [memoranda] dictated. Little or no effort had to be diverted to handling private business or to the machinery of living. All that could be done by others. Even so, a man of lesser stature could have worked equally long and devotedly and have achieved little. I myself worked with or under people whose energy seemed inexhaustible, but who had little to show for it in the end. Energy and stamina are not enough, and it was Churchill's other characteristics which made so great a difference."

I have ever been concerned," ordered the British navy to open fire on their former allies.[135] Two French battleships and a cruiser were sunk. The world had seen for the first time the determination of Britain to win the war.

The Battle of Britain

Hitler was, indeed, preparing to invade Britain. First, however, Germany had to win control of the air and to reduce the capability of Britain to resist. On August 8, 1940, the *Luftwaffe,* the German air force, began bombing British ports. On August 19 it began to bomb airfields and, on September 6, started the two-month-long assault on London known as the blitz.

Hitler hoped the fierce bombing alone would cause Britain to surrender. Instead, the British grew almost cheerful and more determined than ever to triumph. It was Churchill who inspired them. He was everywhere—inspecting the troops, viewing damage, encouraging the people. He was the very symbol of defiance—cigar held tightly in his teeth, fingers flashing the famous "V for victory" sign.

The people loved him. His chief of staff, General Hastings Ismay, described a visit to a shelter where people were taken when their homes had been destroyed by bombs. He mentioned "an old woman who was the picture of misery, pouring her soul into her handkerchief. Suddenly she looked up, saw Winston, and her whole face lit up. She waved her handkerchief and cried: 'Hooray! Hooray! Hooray!'. . .

As Churchill had predicted, with France's surrender to Germany, Britain became Hitler's next target. Hitler used frightening tactics to demoralize the British people, who suffered blistering attacks such as this air raid on London.

Hitler hoped that by bombing London (pictured here in 1941), he would prompt British citizens to advocate their government's surrender. He underestimated the British and Churchill's leadership.

Tears were pouring down his face."[136]

Years later, Churchill was to say that 1940 was "the most splendid, as it was the most deadly, year in our long English and British history."[137] He drove his staff, issuing an endless stream of written orders to those under him. Many were tagged with red labels calling for "Action This Day." Yet, the staff loved him as much as the people did. Sir George Mallaby, a cabinet under-secretary, later wrote:

> Anybody who served anywhere near him was devoted to him. It is hard to say why. He was not kind or considerate. . . . He was exacting beyond reason and ruthlessly critical. He continually exhibited all the characteristics which one usually deplores and abominates in the boss. Not only did he get away with it but nobody really wanted him otherwise. He was unusual, unpredictable, exciting, original, stimulating, provocative, outrageous, uniquely experienced,

abundantly talented, humorous, entertaining—almost everything a man could be, a great man.[138]

Churchill had always loved adventure, and here was his greatest adventure ever. He was still, in many ways, the small boy playing toy soldiers at Blenheim. With bombs falling on London, he would go to the roof of Number 10 Downing Street to see the action. When others tried to persuade him to take shelter, he refused, saying, "I love the bangs."[139]

Against the German onslaught, Britain could send pitifully few squadrons of Royal Air Force (RAF) fighters. The British pilots demonstrated incredible bravery and endurance, returning from a mission and catching only a few hours sleep before taking off once more to meet another wave of German bombers. "Never in the field of human conflict," said Churchill, "was so much owed by so many to so few."[140] By November the Germans had lost a great many

A Firsthand Look

During the German blitz of London in 1940, Churchill frequently inspected the damage in person. In Their Finest Hour, *he described one such visit to a bombed area.*

"Already little pathetic Union Jacks [Britain's flag] had been stuck up amid the ruins. When my car was recognised, the people came running from all quarters, and a crowd of more than a thousand was soon gathered. All these folk were in a high state of enthusiasm. They crowded round us, cheering and manifesting every sign of lively affection, wanting to touch and to stroke my clothes. One would have thought I had brought them some fine substantial benefit which would improve their lot. I was completely undermined and wept. [General Hastings] Ismay, who was with me, records that he heard an old woman say, 'You see, he really cares. He's crying.' They were tears not of sorrow but of wonder and admiration. . . . When we got back into the car, a harsher mood swept over this haggard crowd. 'Give it 'em back,' they cried, and 'Let *them* have it too.' I undertook forthwith to see that their wishes were carried out; and this promise was certainly kept. The debt was repaid tenfold, twentyfold, in the frightful routine bombardment of German cities, which grew in intensity as our air power developed, as the bombs became far heavier and the explosives more powerful. Certainly the enemy got it all back in good measure, pressed down and running over. Alas for poor humanity!"

Churchill visits people living in the burned out remains of London. He vowed to seek revenge on Germany's leader by bombing German cities.

planes and had failed to knock the RAF out of the air. Also, winter was approaching and the weather would not permit an invasion force to cross the English Channel. The bombing continued, but the invasion was, for the moment, called off.

Action in North Africa

Britain had not been entirely on the defensive. In one of his most difficult and important decisions, Churchill had removed troops from Britain, which was expecting an invasion, and sent them to Egypt. Italy had entered the war on Germany's side, and Italian troops in North Africa threatened to capture the Suez Canal, cutting Britain's link with India. The British attacked in December and routed the Italians. This forced the Germans to take troops from France—troops that might have fought against Britain—

and send them to Africa.

Britain cheered the victories in Africa, but Churchill's greatest victory had been won without a shot. Britain was even more vulnerable to attack from beneath the surface of the sea than from the air. Supplies had to reach the island nation by ship, and German submarines were sinking merchant ships at an alarming rate.

Days after war had been declared, Churchill had asked Roosevelt to sell Britain fifty American destroyers to defend against submarines. Roosevelt delayed. For one thing, many members of Congress were opposed to any U.S. involvement. For another, he thought Hitler might defeat Britain and then use the destroyers against the United States.

Churchill's speeches, however, and Britain's determination and courage, convinced Roosevelt that the British would hold out. He agreed to sell the destroyers. The United States would sell Britain other badly needed war matériel, as well. The

A German submarine sinks an Allied tanker. After British ships were equipped with sonar, the tide would turn against Germany's submarines.

The Single Goal

It had always been a trademark of Churchill that when he confronted a problem, it commanded his complete attention. This, wrote John Colville in Action This Day, *was his strength—and that of Britain—during World War II.*

"Strength often marches with simplicity. In the war Churchill's burden was lightened and his task simplified by his refusal to be diverted from the single aim of victory: victory at any price, since the alternative was slavery or extinction. This suited his temperament, because although a brilliant political tactician and more fertile than most men in imagination and ideas, he was fundamentally a straightforward person who eschewed [avoided] devious paths and struck out for goals which he could see. He had little of Lloyd George's cunning or the well-disguised craftiness of Stanley Baldwin. His decisions might be unpredictable, but his motives were seldom hard to fathom, and in forming his opinion of men he would have thought it an impertinence to probe too far beneath the surface. In August 1940 he considered the clamour for a Statement of War Aims ill-conceived. We had, he said, only one aim: to destroy Hitler. Let those who did not know what we were fighting for stop and see for themselves. France was now discovering why she had been fighting, and we, since we must win in order to survive, could only take the short view."

question was: How would Britain pay for it?

Roosevelt sent his most trusted adviser, Harry Hopkins, to meet with Churchill in January 1941. Hopkins was impressed with Churchill and with the British spirit. He told Churchill that the United States would supply Britain's needs in the form of a lease, with payment after the war. At a large dinner Hopkins summed up the commitment of the United States toward Britain with a verse from the Book of Ruth in the Bible: "Whither thou goest, I will go; and where thou lodgest, I will lodge; thy people shall be my people, and thy God my God." Hopkins paused, and then added, "Even unto the end."[141] Churchill wept for joy.

Through the first months of 1941, the British battled Germany in North Africa, Greece, and on the Mediterranean island of Crete. At sea, the Germans were sinking British ships faster than new ones could be built. But the Germans were losing submarines, too. British ships were being equipped with sonar, a device capable of detecting submarines under the water.

Churchill had been an important part of the development of sonar as a member of the National Research Council before the war.

Hitler Turns on the Soviets

In June, Britain gained an ally. Hitler, frustrated in his desire to invade Britain, turned east and attacked the Soviet Union. Churchill immediately promised to give Stalin all the help possible. He offered to ship war matériel to the Soviets, even though such items were in short supply in Britain. Some thought this strange in view of Churchill's well-known hatred of communism, but he said, "If Hitler invaded Hell, I would at least make a favorable reference to the Devil in the House of Commons."[142]

In August, Churchill sailed to Placentia Bay off the coast of Newfoundland in Canada. He was met there by Roosevelt, who agreed to increase American aid to Britain and also to begin sending help to the Soviets. He and Churchill also signed a document that Churchill had written. It was a blueprint for what the world would be like after the war. Among other things, it called for the right of all people to determine their own form of government. The document, the Atlantic Charter, would ultimately become the foundation of the charter of the United Nations.

Meanwhile, the war was not going well for the Allies. The Germans continued to advance in the Soviet Union. Stalin demanded that the British relieve the pressure on the Soviets by landing troops in France or Norway, in order to open a "second front." Churchill refused. He knew Britain was still far too weak. In Africa, the Germans under their brilliant general, Edwin Rommel, pushed the British back toward Egypt.

Nazi troops invade Russia. Hitler turned against his former ally after the Battle of Britain failed.

(Left) The Japanese attack on Pearl Harbor brought the reluctant Americans into the war at last. (Below) President Franklin D. Roosevelt signs the declaration of war on the Axis powers.

America Enters the War

Then, after dinner on Sunday, December 7, 1941, Churchill turned on the radio to hear the news. The announcer spoke about the war in Africa and the Soviet Union, then said that a Japanese attack on the United States had been reported. Churchill quickly put in a call to Roosevelt. "Mr. President," he asked, "what's this about Japan?"

"It's true," said Roosevelt. "They have attacked us at Pearl Harbor [the U.S. Navy base in Hawaii]. We're all in the same boat now."[143]

Thus Churchill's greatest hope, America's entry into the war, was about to be realized. That night, he "slept the sleep of the saved and thankful." He knew in his heart the war was won. He later wrote:

> So, we had won after all! Yes, after Dunkirk; after the fall of France; after the horrible episode of Oran; after the threat of invasion, when, apart from the Air [Force] and the Navy, we were almost an unarmed people; after the deadly struggle of the U-boat [submarine] war . . . we had won the war. England would live; Britain would live.[144]

8 Victory and Defeat

In 1940 and 1941, Winston Churchill's chief concern was the survival of Britain. Once the Soviet Union and the United States had entered the war, his task became to coordinate military operations with his allies. He also was looking ahead at the political shape of the world after the war had been won.

Churchill first feared the United States might put everything into the war against Japan and refrain from taking a major part in the struggle against Germany. Two weeks after the attack on Pearl Harbor, he went to Washington and convinced Roosevelt that every effort should be made to defeat Germany first. On December 26, 1941, Churchill spoke to Congress. He said, "I cannot help reflecting that if my father had been American and my mother British, instead of the other way round, I might have got here on my own. In that case, this would not have been the first time you would have heard my voice."[145]

The war in the Pacific went badly for Britain. On December 10, the battleships *Repulse* and *Prince of Wales* were sunk by Japanese bombers. Churchill, who had dismissed the vulnerability of large ships to air attack, had not provided air support. In January 1942, Japanese troops threatened to take the British outpost at Singapore.

On January 27, Churchill asked the House of Commons for a vote of confidence in the way he was running the war. As the debate ended, he said:

> In no way have I mitigated the sense of danger and impending misfortunes— of a minor character and of a severe character—which still hang over us. But at the same time I avow my confidence, never stronger than at this moment, that we shall bring this conflict to an end in a manner agreeable to the interests of our country, and in a manner agreeable to the future of the world.[146]

The vote in favor of Churchill was 464 to 1. When he heard the news, Roosevelt telegraphed Churchill, "It is fun to be in the same decade with you."[147]

Churchill would need every bit of support. In February, Singapore surrendered. In April, the Japanese landed in the Solomon Islands, within striking distance of Australia. In May, the British lost Burma to the Japanese, and the Americans lost the Philippine Islands. In North Africa, the British were retreating before the Germans.

The Strain of War

Churchill was depressed. His daughter Mary wrote in her diary, "Papa is at a low ebb. He is not too well physically, and he is

At Home in Congress

On December 26, 1941, less than two weeks after the Japanese attacked Pearl Harbor and brought the United States into World War II, Churchill made his first speech before the U.S. Congress. He described it in The Grand Alliance.

"I must confess that I felt quite at home, and more sure of myself than I had sometimes been in the House of Commons. What I said was received with the utmost kindness and attention. . . . I ended thus. . . . 'Five or six years ago it would have been easy, without shedding a drop of blood, for the United States and Great Britain to have insisted on fulfillment of the disarmament clauses of the treaties which Germany signed after the Great War [World War I]. . . . That chance has passed. It is gone. Prodigious hammer-strokes have been needed to bring us together again, or, if you will allow me to use other language, I will say that he must indeed have a blind soul who cannot see that some great purpose and design is being worked out here below, of which we will have the honour to be faithful servants. It is not given to us to peer into the mysteries of the future. Still, I avow my hope and faith, sure and inviolate, that in the days to come the British and American peoples will for their own safety and for the good of all walk together side by side in majesty, in justice, and in peace.' Afterwards . . . the Secret Service men . . . took me back to the White House, where the President, who had listened in, told me I had done quite well."

worn down by the continuous crushing pressure of events."[148] Churchill's health had, indeed, suffered. He was now sixty-seven years old, and the strain of the war was making itself felt.

The Soviet Union was suffering enormous losses, and Stalin, backed by the Americans, renewed his plea for a second front. In addition, Roosevelt's top generals wanted a combined British-American force to cross the English Channel and attack the Germans in France. Churchill still was opposed to a cross-Channel attack. For one thing, he

genuinely thought it would fail—that there were not enough men, supplies, and landing craft available. He was also aware of the danger to his own political position. Another military defeat might destroy Britain's confidence in him, and the resulting loss of morale could be disastrous.

Churchill was looking out for Britain's welfare, as well. Rather than sending troops to France, he preferred fighting in areas where British interests were threatened, such as North Africa or the Middle East. He also had begun to see the danger of postwar domination of eastern Europe by the Soviet Union. The Soviets, when they still had an agreement with Germany, had grabbed Finland, the eastern half of Poland, and the Baltic countries of Lithuania, Latvia, and Estonia. Churchill favored sending British and American troops into imperiled countries such as Hungary, Bulgaria, Czechoslovakia, and Romania, not only to free them from the Germans, but also to save them from the Soviets.

Churchill went to Washington again in June to convince the Americans to attack in North Africa rather than in France. He was extremely persuasive, using all his charm on the American generals and admirals, one of whom said that if Churchill had asked for his favorite watch, he would "cheerfully have surrendered it."[149]

The American generals remained unconvinced. General Dwight Eisenhower said a landing in North Africa could be "the blackest day in history."[150] Roosevelt, however, overruled his generals and the invasion of North Africa, Operation Torch, went forward.

Churchill flew to Moscow to tell Stalin that his hoped-for invasion of France would not happen for at least another year. After a four-hour meeting with the Soviet leader, Churchill said:

> I explained at length with maps and arguments, why we would not do a Second Front. Stalin said he did not agree with our reasons. He argued the other way, and everyone was pretty glum. Finally, he said he did not accept our view, but that we had the right to decide. . . . I asked for plain speaking, and I certainly got it. But if Stalin was bitterly disappointed, he listened patiently to my explanation. He never once raised his voice; never once lost his temper. When I had told him the worst, we both sat in silence for a little. . . ."May God prosper this undertaking," he said.[151]

In the second half of 1942, the tide of war turned in the Allies' favor. The Americans

General Dwight D. Eisenhower with troops in England. Eisenhower disagreed with Roosevelt's decision to attack the Germans in North Africa rather than in France.

won a tremendous naval victory at Midway Island in June. In August, the British halted the Germans in North Africa at the Battle of El Alamein. In October, on the other side of North Africa, the Americans and the British came ashore. In January 1943, a large German force surrendered to the Soviets at Stalingrad, and the rest of the Germans began to retreat. "This is not the end," Churchill warned the British in a radio speech. "It is not even the beginning of the end. But it is, perhaps, the end of the beginning."[152]

Churchill and Roosevelt thought another conference was now necessary. They met in North Africa, at Casablanca, Mo-rocco, in January 1943. Stalin had been invited, but he chose not to leave the Soviet Union. Churchill and Roosevelt agreed that a cross-Channel invasion would again be delayed. Instead, the British and Americans, now close to complete victory in North Africa, would invade Italy. This decision made Stalin extremely suspicious of his allies. He thought Britain and the United States were deliberately staying out of France in the west to allow Germany and the Soviets to exhaust each other in the east.

Shortly after Casablanca, Churchill was seriously ill with pneumonia. While recovering, he delivered a radio broadcast in which he gave his vision of postwar

(Left to right) French North Africa high commissioner Gen. Henri Giraud, Roosevelt, De Gaulle, and Churchill meet in Casablanca in 1943 toward the completion of the North African campaign. Again they decided to delay an attack on France in favor of attacking Italy.

Britain. There would be health insurance for everyone "from the cradle to the grave." Leaders would come from every class, and the government and private enterprise would "pull the national wagon side by side."[153] These were much the same concepts he had fought for thirty years earlier alongside Lloyd George.

In April, American troops moving from the west joined British troops coming from the east, and the war in North Africa was at an end. The Americans, however, were having second thoughts about invading Italy. They said they needed all their landing craft in the Pacific.

In May, Churchill sailed for Washington to urge Roosevelt in person not to abandon the Italian campaign. Churchill hoped that the Americans and British could move up through Italy into eastern Europe, getting there before the Soviet Union. On the voyage, he demonstrated that his spirit of adventure remained strong. He ordered a machine gun placed in the lifeboat he would use in case the ship were sunk by a

U.S. troops land in North Africa. The Germans were successfully run out of North Africa in April 1943.

German submarine. "I won't be captured," he said. "The finest way to die is in the excitement of fighting the enemy."[154] In Washington, his personality once more won out, and Roosevelt agreed to the Italian plan.

Allied tanks invade Italy in July 1943. The invasion did not go as quickly as Churchill and Roosevelt had hoped.

A Setback in Italy

The invasion of Italy in the summer of 1943 did not go well. American troops succeeded in taking the island of Sicily, and the British and Americans at first made rapid progress on the mainland of Italy. The Italian government surrendered on September 1, but German troops poured in from the north and slowed the Allied advance to a crawl.

Churchill and Roosevelt met again in August, this time in Canada, at Quebec. Churchill, for the first time, committed Britain to a cross-Channel invasion of France in 1944. He was growing more and more worried that the Soviets would dominate Europe after the war and suggested to Roosevelt that another conference with Stalin was in order.

The conference was scheduled for November in Teheran, the capital of Iran. Just before meeting Stalin, Churchill and Roosevelt conferred in Cairo, Egypt. Churchill argued that the Italian campaign should have priority over the invasion of France. Roosevelt wanted to wait until talking with Stalin before reaching a decision.

At Teheran, Churchill pushed for an advance north through Italy and then east. Stalin, however, did not want British or American troops in any position to threaten his postwar plans for eastern Europe. Roosevelt sided completely with Stalin, and Churchill was forced to accept a date in 1944, for Operation Overlord, as the proposed invasion of France was named. Furthermore, the Soviets were to be allowed to keep the Baltic states and eastern Poland.

The Teheran conference marked a turning point in world affairs. The United States

A wounded U.S. soldier receives first aid in Sicily during the invasion of Italy. Although the Italian government surrendered, the arrival of German troops slowed the Allied victory.

A Mental Toughness

Churchill's long political career, with all its triumphs and defeats, prepared him for the greater triumphs and defeats Britain experienced during World War II. Sir Ian Jacob wrote about this side of Churchill in Action This Day.

"His mental courage was remarkable to me in this way. He was quite impervious to depression, despair, or indeed to the sinking of morale which assails people when the news is constantly bad and disaster looms ahead. He equally did not show much elation when great victories began to come our way. This did not mean that he was insensitive, far from it, but he had tremendous fibre and toughness. His whole life was one long series of ups and downs, and few men could have had so wide an experience of physical danger and also political vicissitude [changes]. He had admitted that he felt that he was capable and equipped to shoulder the supreme responsibility which came to him when he became prime Minister, and this feeling no doubt bore him up. He more than anyone could 'meet with triumph and disaster, and treat those two impostors just the same' [the author is quoting from Rudyard Kipling's poem, "If"]. He was aided, I feel sure, by his great sense of history, and his somewhat old-fashioned ardour for fame. He had more than a touch of the spirit that so inspired [Lord Horatio] Nelson [the British admiral who defeated the French and Spanish fleets at the Battle of Trafalgar in 1805], a spirit of expression which seems to us nowadays slightly embarrassing. But this spirit, while not spurious [phony], can be a real inspiration. There was no trace of vanity about him, and that can be said of few men whose lives have been spent in politics."

and the Soviet Union were clearly the dominant powers. Stalin and Roosevelt made the important decisions. Churchill was, as one historian put it, now little more than "Roosevelt's lieutenant."[155] Roosevelt knew that Churchill was trying to preserve the British Empire, but he did not realize that Stalin was trying to create an empire for the Soviets. In a conversation with his son Elliott, Roosevelt said, "It's a pleasure working with Stalin. There's nothing devious."[156]

Churchill returned to Britain to help coordinate the planning of Overlord, the command of which had been given to General Eisenhower. As usual, when finally committed to a project, he entered into it wholeheartedly. One of his most important contributions to Overlord was the Mulberry, a huge, floating concrete harbor that could be towed across the Channel, anchored, and visited by ships to unload war matériel.

A Fountain of Ideas

Throughout the war, Churchill had been a steady fountain of ideas. "He has a hundred ideas a day," said Roosevelt, "of which four are good."[157] Some, like the Mulberry harbors, the dropping of tinfoil from aircraft to confuse enemy radar, and an oil pipeline under the English Channel, were very good indeed. Others were not. But a key difference between Churchill and Hitler was that Churchill would,

grudgingly, allow himself to be talked out of wilder schemes. No one dared say "no" to Hitler, and Germany suffered for it.

As the day for the liberation of France approached, Churchill, still seeking to be where the action was, wanted to sail with the invaders, who would be landing on June 6, 1944. Eisenhower tried to stop him, but Churchill maintained that he still had command over the British ships and would make himself part of a crew. Churchill finally stayed behind, but only at the request of King George VI.

During the second half of 1944, the British and Americans pushed east and the Soviets advanced from the east. Churchill, afraid Stalin's troops would occupy and dominate all of eastern Europe, proposed to Stalin that the British and Americans have a part in restoring the governments of countries liberated from the Germans.

In what would be the toughest invasion of the war, Allied troops land on the shores of Normandy in 1944.

A visibly ill Roosevelt (center) meets with Churchill and Stalin at Yalta. In spite of Churchill's warnings, Roosevelt agreed to Stalin's demands in Eastern Europe.

Stalin promised not to swallow up his European neighbors.

Stalin's promise, however, was quickly broken. All over eastern Europe, the Soviets installed Communist governments. Many of those who protested were imprisoned or shot. Most of these countries were beyond Churchill's reach, but one—Greece—he was determined to save. He flew to Athens on Christmas Eve 1944, and persuaded the king of Greece to unite with a political enemy, Archbishop Damaskinos, against the Communists. Churchill's private secretary, Sir Leslie Rowan, later wrote that "Greece would not have been a free country had it not been for Churchill's courage and grasp of the essential."[158]

In February 1945, Churchill, Stalin, and Roosevelt met once more, this time at the Soviet city of Yalta on the Crimean Sea. Roosevelt, who had barely two months to live, was very ill. Despite Churchill's warnings, the American president sided with Stalin on every question. Stalin's only concession was a promise that "free elections" would be held in Poland.

Over the next few weeks, it was evident that Stalin's idea of a free election was a vote delayed until all opposition had been silenced. Anyone opposed to the Communists was rounded up and arrested. In April, Churchill wrote to Stalin:

There is not much comfort in looking into a future where you and the countries you dominate, plus the Communist Parties in many other states, are all drawn up on one side, and those who rally to the English-speaking nations . . . are on the other. It is quite obvious that their quarrel would tear the world to pieces, and that all of us leading men on either side who had anything to do with that would be shamed before history. Even embarking on a long period of suspicions, or abuse and counter abuse . . . would be a disaster.[159]

Churchill during a campaign tour in 1945. In spite of all Churchill had accomplished during World War II, the fickle British did not reelect him after the war.

Churchill at the Front

The conquest of Germany was almost complete. In March, British troops crossed the Rhine River into Germany. Churchill visited the front and actually crossed the river himself. German shells began falling and British generals implored him to return to safety, but Churchill refused to budge, wrapping his arms around part of a ruined bridge. "The look on Winston's face," wrote an observer, "was just like that of a small boy being called away from his sand castles on the beach by his nurse."[160]

On April 29, 1945, Adolf Hitler committed suicide in his underground Berlin bunker as what remained of his army battled the Soviets in the streets above. On May 7, Germany surrendered. The next day, Churchill received a standing ovation in the House of Commons. "This is your victory," he said. "It is the victory of the cause of freedom in every land. In all our long history we have never seen a greater day than this. God bless you all."[161]

Churchill always seemed to have a clearer view of the future than any one around him. Now he sounded a warning even as Britain celebrated. He told the cabinet, "There is still a lot to do to make sure that the words 'freedom,' 'democracy,' and 'liberation' are not distorted from their true meaning as we have come to know them."[162] He wrote to Harry Truman, who had become president of the United States upon Roosevelt's death in April, "What is to happen about Russia? The Iron Curtain is drawn down upon their front."[163] It was Churchill's first use of what was to become a famous phrase.

With the war in Europe over, the Labour

Party insisted on a general election, the first in Britain in ten years. Churchill counted on his personal popularity to keep the Conservatives in power. Instead of concentrating on his accomplishments, however, he attacked the Labour Party, warning that they would bring "some form of Gestapo" (the Nazi secret police).[164]

The British working people distrusted the Conservatives. They never forgot that the "men of Munich," who had appeased their way into World War II, had been Conservatives. Now, their old antagonism toward Churchill was renewed. The ghosts of Tonypandy and the *British Gazette* returned to haunt him. The election was an overwhelming victory for the Labour Party, which won a majority in the House of Commons of almost two hundred seats.

The Shock of Defeat

Churchill was shocked and hurt. Determined "not to remain for an hour responsible for the country's affairs," he went to the king on the day the results were announced and handed in his resignation.[165] The Labour Party leader, Clement Attlee, would be the new prime minister.

Publicly, Churchill accepted the verdict of the people. "They are perfectly entitled to vote for whom they please," he told an aide. "This is democracy. This is what we have been fighting for."[166] Privately, he was bitter, saying, "No sooner was the peril over than they turned me out."[167] Clementine tried to console him and said that perhaps the election was a blessing in disguise. "At the moment," Churchill answered, "it seems quite effectively disguised."[168]

King George tried to soften the blow, offering to induct Churchill into the Order of the Garter, the highest honor Britain can bestow on an individual. Churchill declined. "I could not accept the Order of the Garter from my Sovereign," he wrote, "when I had received the order of the boot from his people."[169] Once more, it appeared that Churchill's career had come to an end. No one, Churchill least of all, suspected that two more decades of service lay ahead.

9 Elder Statesman

When the Conservatives lost the 1945 election and Winston Churchill was no longer prime minister, most thought he must surely retire. He was, after all, seventy years old. Yet, his motto was "Never give in." He announced he would remain the leader of the Conservative opposition.

For weeks, however, Churchill's "Black Dog" of depression hung about. "It would have been better to have been killed in an airplane accident or died like Roosevelt," he told his doctor.[170] When a secretary remarked that now he had time to rest, Churchill muttered, "No, I wanted to do the peace, too."[171]

He and daughter Sarah went on a trip to Italy. Just as in 1915, painting cheered him up. He had done only one picture during the entire war. Now, he painted three within one week. "I paint all day & every day," he wrote to his daughter Mary, "& have banished care & disillusionment to the shades."[172] To his wife, he wrote about the problems facing the new government and confessed that "It may all, indeed, be 'a blessing in disguise.'"[173]

He did not remain away from world affairs long. On his return to Britain, he found an invitation from President Truman to speak at Westminster College in Fulton, Missouri. Churchill used the occasion to begin warning the world about the threat of communism. On March 5, 1946, he told his audience:

From Stettin in the Baltic to Trieste in the Adriatic, an iron curtain has descended across the Continent. Behind that line lie all the capitals of the ancient states of Central and Eastern Europe. Warsaw, Berlin, Prague, Vienna, Budapest, Belgrade, Bucharest and Sofia, all these famous cities and the

Churchill paints in Italy after World War II. He and his daughter Sarah took a trip there after Churchill failed to regain his position as prime minister.

Churchill gives his Iron Curtain speech in the United States in 1946. Churchill's predictions about communism would prove deadly accurate.

populations around them lie in what I must call the Soviet sphere, and all are subject in one form or another, not only to Soviet influence but to a very high, and, in many cases, increasing measure of control from Moscow. . . . Police governments are prevailing in nearly every case. . . . These are somber facts for anyone to have to recite on the morrow of victory gained by so much splendid comradeship in arms and in the cause of freedom and democracy; but we should be most unwise not to face them squarely while time remains.[174]

Another Unwelcome Warning

Churchill knew his message would be no more welcome in 1946 than his warnings about Hitler had been in the 1930s. "Last time I saw it coming and cried aloud to my own fellow-countrymen and to the world," he said at Fulton, "but no one paid any attention." This time, he vowed, he would be heard, observing that another disaster could be prevented "by reaching now, in 1946, a good understanding on all points with Russia."[175]

In the 1930s Churchill had been a discredited politician. Now, however, he was the most distinguished statesman in the world. When he spoke, people listened. One historian wrote that "no speech by a politician out of office and power has exerted such an influence on events. For it is to this that we must date the alerting of the democracies to their danger and the mental preparedness to take steps in their own defence."[176]

Stalin's reaction to what became known as the Iron Curtain speech was to say that it was "calculated to sow the seeds of discord" and that Churchill was "now in the position of a warmonger."[177] Nevertheless, he announced that he would, after all, keep his promise to withdraw Soviet troops from northern Iran.

Although Communists in the United States loudly demonstrated against Churchill, Truman was convinced that his visitor was correct. In 1947 the president announced the Truman Doctrine. The United States, he said, would defend "free people . . . against aggressive movements that seek to impose upon them totalitarian régimes."[178] A year later, in 1948, Britain, France, the United States, and several other countries signed the Atlantic Pact, which led to the creation of the North Atlantic Treaty Organization (NATO) to defend against possible Soviet aggression.

Churchill, however, had fought in two wars and led his country through a third. Rather than war, he wanted to achieve peace with the Soviet Union, but he knew—as the appeasers in Britain in the 1930s had not—that the key to peace was strength. In a 1949 speech in New York, he said:

> You have not only to convince the Soviet government that you have superior force—that they are confronted by superior force—but that you are not restrained by any moral consideration, if the case arose, from using that force with complete material ruthlessness. And that is the greatest chance of peace, the surest road to peace. Then, the Communists will make a bargain.[179]

Churchill was by no means totally occupied with international affairs. In Britain, he led Conservative protests against the Labour Party program of nationalizing

Keeping a Stiff Upper Lip

If Churchill was bitter about the election defeat in 1945, he hid it from some of his closest associates. In Action This Day, *Sir Leslie Rowan, his private secretary, recalled the day of the defeat, and Churchill's reaction.*

"Of course, Churchill was greatly disappointed that at his moment of triumph he was rejected; I saw him perhaps more that day than any other official, and it was one of the saddest days of my life. I was certainly very bitter, but not so Churchill. No single word of condemnation passed his lips; this was the working of the system, and he accepted it. Indeed he would have said that it was precisely this freedom of choice for which we had fought. But for him the system was not merely Parliament; it was also the Civil Service; for he said to me, immediately he was back from his resignation visit to the Palace, 'you must not think of me any more; your duty is now to serve [Labour Party leader Clement] Attlee, if he wishes you to do so. You must therefore go to him, for you must also think of your future.' I am bound to confess that I broke down and cried, but obeyed."

(bringing under government control) some of the most important industries. The destruction of private enterprise, Churchill told the House of Commons, would bring economic disaster to Britain. He said the government's "insatiable lust for power is only equaled by their incurable impotence in exercising it."[180]

Indian Freedom, Israeli Statehood

In 1947 Churchill played key roles in finally settling two problems that had bothered both him and Britain for decades. He was opposed, as always, to the end of British rule in India. Yet, on July 4, he led the Conservatives in their support of the Indian Independence Bill. Also that year, at Churchill's urging, the issue of Palestine went before the United Nations, leading to the foundation of the Jewish state of Israel.

Churchill found plenty of time for a personal life as well as a public one. As always, he used his time out of office to write. During the 1930s, even as he thundered against Hitler, he was writing his highly acclaimed biography of his ancestor John Churchill, the first duke of Marlborough. Now, his subject was World War II. Aided by hordes of researchers and secretaries, he began what would ultimately be a six-volume history of the war.

Churchill and Clementine also were hard at work restoring Chartwell, their country home. During the war, Churchill had spent most of his time in London or at Chequers, the official country home of the prime minister. Chartwell had been neglected and now had to be attended to. He

Churchill (right) and a friend outside Chartwell in 1949. Churchill used his time out of office to work on his country estate and even to take up horseback riding.

bought five hundred acres close to Chartwell so that he could start a farm. He even bought racehorses, much to Clementine's dismay. "Before he bought the horse (I cannot think why)," she wrote to a friend, "he had hardly been on a racecourse in his life. I must say I don't find it madly amusing."[181]

By 1949 the Labour government was declining in popularity. The British economy had not responded to the new policy of nationalization. In fact, meat, sugar, and many other day-to-day items were still rationed, as they had been during the war. Before the country could turn even more strongly against him, the prime minister, Clement Attlee, called an election for February.

During the campaign, Churchill told the voters they had a choice "whether we should take another plunge into Socialist regimentation, or by a strong effort, regain the freedom, initiative and opportunity of British life."[182] The Labour Party remained in power, but its majority was a bare six seats.

Prime Minister Once More

Only eighteen months later, in a worsening economy, Attlee called another election. The Labour Party attacked Churchill as an adventurer who would get Britain into another war, but Churchill had learned his lesson from the 1945 campaign. Instead of attacking his opponents, he emphasized what the Conservatives would do if elected. The voting took place on October 25, 1951, and the Conservatives won a majority in the House of Commons of twenty-six seats. Only a month before his seventy-seventh birthday, Churchill was once again prime minister of Great Britain.

His second term of office was not a great success. Internationally, he tried to bring about a united Europe, which might someday include even the Soviet Union. His efforts failed, in part because France was unwilling to enter into any kind of a partnership with Germany. He also wanted to hold a meeting with the American and Soviet leaders to help end what was now known as the Cold War. This opportunity was refused by Dwight Eisenhower, now president of the United States, and his secretary of state, John Foster Dulles.

At home, the economy improved, but very slowly. The biggest boost for British morale was the coronation in 1953 of Queen Elizabeth II. In a broadcast, Churchill said,

Churchill campaigning in 1950. He became prime minister of Great Britain for a second time in 1951.

The Wound of Defeat

When Churchill was forced to resign as prime minister in 1945, it was a bitter blow to the man who had led Britain to victory in World War II. His doctor, a year later, made this entry in his diary, quoted in Churchill: Taken from the Diaries of Lord Moran.

"When a man is in the seventies, he throws off the effects of a surgical operation very slowly, very imperfectly. He appears to recover, but things are not the same as they were, and in the end his life may be shortened. The result of the General Election last summer left a mark on Winston which I can only liken to the scar of a major operation. It is true that he came safely out of the hospital and went abroad for a period of convalescence, and that now he has come back ready for work. But it is a different Winston. The supreme self-confidence of the war years has been undermined, something of the old *élan* [high spirit] has evaporated. The wound appears to have healed, but there is left an ugly scar. Winston—incredible as it may seem—is out of a job, looking for something to do, anything to keep his mind away from the past. . . . 'There are lots of flies buzzing round this old decaying carcass. I want something to keep them away. . . . I think I can be of some use over there [the United States]. It may be that Congress will ask me to address them. . . . It's a funny position. I feel I could do things and there's nothing to be done.'"

"I, whose youth was passed in the august, unchallenged, and tranquil glories of the Victorian Era, may well feel a thrill in invoking, once more, the prayer and Anthem: 'God Save the Queen.'"[183] Elizabeth, the next year, was to renew her father's offer to make Churchill a Knight of the Garter. This time, he would accept, to be known henceforth as "Sir Winston."

Churchill's health, however, was failing. "The bright and sparkling intervals still come, and they are still unequaled," wrote his private secretary, John Colville, "but age is beginning to show."[184] He had had a mild stroke in 1949 and, on June 23, 1953, suffered a much more serious one. The extent of his illness was kept secret from all but a few of his closest colleagues. He was out of Parliament for four months.

In October 1953 Churchill received one of his greatest honors, the Nobel Prize in literature. Between *The Malakand Field Force* in 1898 and *A History of the English-Speaking Peoples* in 1956, he published more than forty books and hundreds of magazine articles. His books alone totaled more than three million words. His multivolume *History of the Second World War* remains the most valuable, unique in that it is the only book on the war written by one who was head of a major power.

Churchill recovered from his stroke and returned to Parliament, but he wasn't the same. The *New York Times* said, "This was not the Churchill of two years ago and was only a shadow of the great figure of 1940."[185] Even members of his cabinet urged him to resign, but he clung to office and, indeed, seemed to grow stronger. His doctor wrote, "This astonishing creature obeys no laws, recognizes no rules."[186]

Finally, he yielded. On March 30, 1955, the eighty-year-old Churchill asked foreign minister Anthony Eden and chancellor of the exchequer R.A. Butler to visit him. "I am going," he said after a short silence. "Anthony will succeed me. We can discuss the details later."[187]

On April 4, Churchill was driven to Buckingham Palace to formally submit his resignation to Queen Elizabeth. She praised his lifetime of service and offered to make him a duke. That, however, would have put Churchill in the House of Lords. "I said that I would like to go on in the Commons while I felt physically fit," he wrote.[188]

Twilight

The last ten years of Churchill's life were peaceful. He continued to paint and to write, to occupy his seat in Parliament, and to follow politics and world affairs closely. As the years went by, more and more honors came to him. In 1958 Churchill College was established at Cambridge University. He was given the honorary post of Lord Warden of the Cinque [Five] Ports, a title traditionally granted to the person acknowledged to be the greatest living Englishman.

Each year, on the opening of Parliament, he entered the House of Commons in a wheelchair and walked to his seat, to a standing ovation. In the House chamber, an arch, rebuilt from the rubble left by Hitler's bombers in 1940, was named Churchill Arch. At last, in 1963, Churchill announced that he would not seek reelection. "I cannot tell you with what sadness I feel constrained to take this step," he said to the House. "I have had the honour and privilege of sitting in the House of Commons for more than sixty years. . . . Among the many aspects and chapters of my public life, it is my tenure as Member of Parliament that I value most highly."[189]

In the same year, 1963, Churchill became the first person ever to be awarded honorary U.S. citizenship by an act of Congress. Randolph Churchill accepted the proclamation from President John F. Kennedy as his father watched on television in London. In a letter to Kennedy, Churchill wrote, "Our past is the key to our future, which I firmly trust and believe will be no less fertile and glorious. Let no man underrate our energies, our potentialities and our abiding power for good."[190]

On November 30, 1964, his ninetieth birthday, Churchill appeared at the upstairs window of his London home. As a crowd cheered below, he flashed the old "V for victory" sign. On January 10, 1965, he suffered a massive stroke. On January 24, seventy years to the day after the death of his father, Winston Churchill died peacefully in his sleep.

Londoners by the thousands, when they heard the announcement, went to Trafalgar Square to stand in silence.

Father of the House

In the 1960s, Churchill was the oldest member of Parliament. Despite being nearly ninety years of age and very feeble, he went to the House of Commons whenever possible. This excerpt from an article by Edwin Roth of the Vancouver Times *describing one of the last visits— February 27, 1964— is found in* Man of the Century, *compiled by the* Reader's Digest.

"The big, swinging doors opposite the press gallery are opened wide by two tail-coated messengers. Just behind the wide open swing doors stands a wheelchair. Two Tory Members of Parliament, conscious of the great honor, help Sir Winston Churchill rise to his feet. As always he wears an elegant black jacket with striped trousers, and his famous black butterfly tie with white spots. A large white handkerchief protrudes from his breast pocket, and a golden watch chain curls across his waistcoat. His bald head with its wisps of snowy hair still seems enormous, and his wrinkled face is rosy. Slowly, one short step at a time, the two members help the Father of the House into the Chamber. His right hand clutches at a stick on which he leans heavily. He pauses and bows respectfully to the Speaker, as all Members do when they enter, then very shakily walks to his seat at the corner of the first row of Conservative benches. All eyes in the Chamber watch this proud, brave and poignant walk until the moment when Sir Winston sinks down on the green leather, grateful that the walk is over again— and pleased that he has made it. . . . When Sir Winston has had enough he begins to pick up his stick. Immediately two Members walk over to help him up. If he is not too tired Sir Winston growls proudly that he wants to walk alone—and he walks alone with his stick. Sometimes his left leg, still held by a surgical pin [from an operation for a broken hip], cannot take the strain, and helping hands must support him. At the Bar of the House, Sir Winston turns slowly, and bows to Mr. Speaker. For long moments, he looks at the Chamber, as though he were reviewing his life. As the two tail-coated messengers open the big swing doors, the waiting wheelchair is seen."

Final Tributes

Although they had frequently failed to listen to him and had often voted against him, the ordinary people of Great Britain knew how much they owed Churchill. Sir Leslie Rowan, in Action This Day, *gave this picture of how they paid their last respects after Churchill's death in 1965.*

"This [Rowan's essay] is merely a short account of how I saw Churchill as a man; it is not an attempt to analyse his war policy or his place in history, national or international. Time and others will do that. But his place, as a man, in the hearts of all Britons was surely established beyond doubt by his last journey of all, to St. Paul's, on the River Thames and finally to Bladon churchyard. On that last journey by train from Waterloo [Station] to Bladon, after the great crowds of London, two single figures whom I saw from the carriage window epitomised [typified] for me what Churchill really meant to ordinary people; first on the flat roof of a small house a man standing at attention in his old R.A.F. uniform, saluting; and then in a field, some hundreds of yards away from the track, a simple farmer stopping work and standing, head bowed, and cap in hand."

More than a million people turned out to watch Churchill's funeral cortege wind its way from Westminster Abbey to St. Paul's Cathedral. As Churchill had requested, the procession was accompanied by "lots of soldiers and bands."

Churchill's coffin is carried up the steps of St. Paul's. The queen had ordered that Churchill be given a state funeral.

Queen Elizabeth ordered that Churchill be given a state funeral, the first held for a commoner in almost seventy years. For three days his body lay in state in Westminster Abbey, one of Britain's national shrines—the site of coronations, and the resting place of monarchs and distinguished citizens. More than 300,000 people paid their respects, including—in a break with tradition—the queen herself.

The Final Journey

Churchill had left instructions for his funeral. It came as no surprise to anyone who had known him that he wanted "lots of soldiers and bands."[191] When the day arrived, more than a million people lined the streets as the procession wound from Westminster Abbey to St. Paul's Cathedral. The final hymn, as Churchill had requested, was American—the *Battle Hymn of the Republic*.

After the funeral service, the coffin and the family were taken by special train to the village of Bladon, within sight of Blenheim Palace. There, Churchill was buried next to his mother and father.

The world had lost one of its truly heroic figures. Tributes poured in from every nation, from those who had fought both with and against him in politics and in war. Perhaps the most stirring was given by an American, former Illinois governor and Democratic presidential nominee Adlai E. Stevenson, who said:

> Like the grandeur and power of masterpieces of art and music, Churchill's life uplifts our hearts and fills us with fresh revelation of the scale and reach of human achievement. . . . We shall hear no longer the remembered eloquence and wit, the old courage and defiance, the robust serenity of indomitable faith. Our world is thus poorer, our political dialogue diminished, and the sources of public inspiration run more thinly for us all. There is a lonesome place against the sky.[192]

Man of the Century

When the twentieth century is over and its history written, it would be surprising if the central figure to emerge were not Winston Churchill. He dominated the first half of the century in a way matched by no one else. His influence, likewise, has filled the second half.

His contributions in many fields—in warfare as the father of the tank, modernizer of the navy, and early advocate of air power; in the betterment of humanity as the author of social legislation; in literature as a historian of the first rank—would qualify him for greatness. However, all these accomplishments, important as they are, fade into the background before one overwhelming fact: Churchill saved democracy—certainly once, and perhaps twice.

Churchill himself, though never one to be modest, might have denied this. In 1954, on his eightieth birthday, he said, "It was the nation and the race dwelling all round the world that had the lion's heart. I had the luck to be called on to give the roar."[193]

It was more than luck. One of Churchill's most severe critics, A.J.P. Taylor, wrote that despite many shortcomings, "the fact remains that [Churchill] won the Second World War."[194] His leadership, his speeches, and his unconquerable willpower brought

Churchill inspects British troops in 1940. Historians agree that Churchill's unflagging willpower and stirring speeches won the Battle of Britain.

Britain back from the brink of defeat in 1940. No one else could have done it. A cabinet colleague that year wrote that Churchill was "the man, and the only man we have for this task."[195]

What Might Have Been

Had Britain surrendered to Hitler, the Germans would have been free to concentrate their entire might against the Soviet Union and very likely would have won. Then, as A.L. Rowse projected, "A German victory would leave America unprepared and exposed to a hostile Europe on the Atlantic front, when she already had a hostile Japan facing her across the Pacific."[196] The result might well have been a postwar world dominated by Germany and Japan.

Once more, in 1946, it was Churchill's voice that warned the free world against Stalin and the intentions of the Soviet Union. His voice was heeded, and steps were taken to halt the spread of communism.

Despite his love of action and adventure, Churchill was not a lover of war. He did not want another conflict. In 1947 he said:

> Let there be sunshine on both sides of the Iron Curtain; and if ever the sunshine should be equal on both sides, the Curtain will be no more. It will vanish away like the mists of morning and melt in the warm light of happy days and cheerful friendship.[197]

Winston Churchill was a man of remarkable talents—a writer, painter, statesman, warrior, and gifted speaker. He remains one of the most important men of the twentieth century.

Thanks largely to Churchill, the free world closed ranks against communism in the 1940s and, twenty-five years after his death, the Iron Curtain disintegrated.

Few people have both the ability and the opportunity to affect the course of history. Winston Churchill used his talents to make the most of his opportunity and thus deserves to be called, in the words of a political foe, Clement Attlee, "the greatest Englishman of our time—I think the greatest citizen of the world of our time."[198]

Notes

Introduction: Man of Destiny

1.   Quoted in Martin Gilbert, *Churchill: A Life*. New York: Henry Holt, 1992.

2.   Quoted in William Manchester, *Visions of Glory: 1874-1932*. New York: Dell, 1983.

3.   Lord Normanbrook, quoted in John Wheeler-Bennett, ed., *Action This Day*. London: St. Martin's Press, 1969.

4.   Quoted in Charles Wilson (Lord Moran), *Churchill: Taken from the Diaries of Lord Moran*. Boston: Houghton Mifflin, 1966.

5.   William Manchester, *Alone: 1932-1940*. New York: Dell, 1988.

6.   Wilson (Lord Moran), *Churchill: Taken from the Diaries of Lord Moran*.

Chapter 1: The Naughtiest Boy in the World

7.   Randolph S. Churchill, *Winston S. Churchill, Vol. I, Youth, 1874-1900*. Boston: Houghton Mifflin, 1966.

8.   Quoted in Manchester, *Visions of Glory*.

9.   Winston S. Churchill, *My Early Life*. New York: Scribner's/Macmillan, 1987.

10.   Winston S. Churchill, *My Early Life*.

11.   Winston S. Churchill, *My Early Life*.

12.   Quoted in Ralph G. Martin, *Jennie, the Life of Lady Randolph Churchill: The Romantic Years, 1854-1895*. Englewood Cliffs, NJ: Prentice Hall, 1969.

13.   Winston S. Churchill, *My Early Life*.

14.   Quoted in Randolph S. Churchill, *Winston S. Churchill, Vol. I, Youth*.

15.   Quoted in Randolph S. Churchill, *Winston S. Churchill, Vol. I, Youth*.

16.   Quoted in Randolph S. Churchill, *Winston S. Churchill, Vol. I, Youth*.

17.   Quoted in Randolph S. Churchill, *Winston S. Churchill, Vol. I, Youth*.

18.   Winston S. Churchill, *My Early Life*.

19.   Winston S. Churchill, *My Early Life*.

20.   Randolph S. Churchill, *Winston S. Churchill, Vol. I, Youth*.

21.   Winston S. Churchill, *My Early Life*.

22.   Winston S. Churchill, *My Early Life*.

23.   Quoted in Manchester, *Visions of Glory*.

24.   Quoted in Randolph S. Churchill, *Winston S. Churchill, Vol. I, Youth*.

25.   Winston S. Churchill, *My Early Life*.

26.   Quoted in Manchester, *Visions of Glory*.

27.   Winston S. Churchill, *My Early Life*.

28.   Winston S. Churchill, *My Early Life*.

29.   Winston S. Churchill, *My Early Life*.

30.   Winston S. Churchill, *My Early Life*.

Chapter 2: Soldier, Writer, Politician

31.   Quoted in Randolph S. Churchill, *Winston S. Churchill, Vol. I, Youth*.

32.   Quoted in Manchester, *Visions of Glory*.

33.   From the *Times* (London), quoted in Randolph S. Churchill, *Winston S. Churchill, Vol. I, Youth*.

34.   Winston S. Churchill, *My Early Life*.

35.   Quoted in Martin Gilbert, *Churchill: A Life*.

36.   Winston S. Churchill, *My Early Life*.

37.   Quoted in Manchester, *Visions of Glory*.

38.   Quoted in Victor L. Albjerg, *Winston Churchill*. New York: Twayne, 1973.

39.   Quoted in Manchester, *Visions of Glory*.

40.   Quoted in Gilbert, *Churchill: A Life*.

41.   Quoted in Manchester, *Visions of Glory*.

42.   Quoted in Kay Halle, *Irrepressible Churchill*. Cleveland, OH: World, 1966.

43.   Quoted in Violet Bonham Carter, *Winston Churchill: An Intimate Portrait*. New York: Harcourt, Brace & World, 1965.

44. Winston S. Churchill, *My Early Life*.

45. Quoted in Winston S. Churchill, *My Early Life*.

46. Manchester, *Visions of Glory*.

Chapter 3: Conservative to Liberal

47. Quoted in Manchester, *Visions of Glory*.

48. Quoted from *Vanity Fair*, in Gilbert, *Churchill: A Life*.

49. Quoted in Gilbert, *Churchill: A Life*.

50. Quoted in Halle, *Irrepressible Churchill*.

51. A.L. Rowse, *The Churchills: The Story of a Family*. New York: Harper & Row, 1966.

52. Robert Rhodes James, *Churchill: A Study in Failure*. New York: World, 1970.

53. Quoted in Bonham Carter, *Winston Churchill: An Intimate Portrait*.

54. Quoted in James, *Churchill: A Study in Failure*.

55. Quoted in Albjerg, *Winston Churchill*.

56. James, *Churchill: A Study in Failure*.

57. Quoted in Manchester, *Visions of Glory*.

58. Quoted in James, *Churchill: A Study in Failure*.

59. James, *Churchill: A Study in Failure*.

60. Bonham Carter, *Winston Churchill: An Intimate Portrait*.

61. Quoted in Manchester, *Visions of Glory*.

62. Quoted in Bonham Carter, *Winston Churchill: An Intimate Portrait*.

Chapter 4: From the Admiralty to the Trenches

63. Rowse, *The Churchills*.

64. Quoted in A.J.P. Taylor, Robert Rhodes James, J.H. Plumb, Basil Liddell Hart, and Anthony Storr, *Churchill Revised*. New York: Dial Press, 1969.

65. Quoted in Manchester, *Visions of Glory*.

66. Quoted in Albjerg, *Winston Churchill*.

67. James, in Taylor, et al., *Churchill Revised*.

68. Quoted in Rowse, *The Churchills*.

69. James, *Churchill: A Study in Failure*.

70. Quoted in Manchester, *Visions of Glory*.

71. Quoted in Bonham Carter, *Winston Churchill: An Intimate Portrait*.

72. Quoted in Manchester, *Visions of Glory*.

73. Quoted in Manchester, *Visions of Glory*.

74. Quoted in Albjerg, *Winston Churchill*.

75. Edward Grigg, quoted in Manchester, *Visions of Glory*.

76. Bonham Carter, *Winston Churchill: An Intimate Portrait*.

77. Quoted in Manchester, *Visions of Glory*.

78. Sir Edward Marsh, quoted in Gilbert, *Churchill: A Life*.

79. Quoted in Albjerg, *Winston Churchill*.

80. Quoted in Gilbert, *Churchill: A Life*.

81. Erich Ludendorff, quoted in Gilbert, *Churchill: A Life*.

82. Quoted in Gilbert, *Churchill: A Life*.

Chapter 5: Back to the Conservatives

83. Quoted in Manchester, *Visions of Glory*.

84. Quoted in Albjerg, *Winston Churchill*.

85. Quoted in Geoffrey Bocca, *The Adventurous Life of Winston Churchill*. New York: Julian Messner, 1958.

86. Quoted in Manchester, *Visions of Glory*.

87. Quoted in Manchester, *Visions of Glory*.

88. Quoted in Gilbert, *Churchill: A Life*.

89. Austen Chamberlain, quoted in Manchester, *Visions of Glory*.

90. Rowse, *The Churchills*.

91. Quoted in Gilbert, *Churchill: A Life*.

92. Quoted in Gilbert, *Churchill: A Life*.

93. Quoted in Halle, *Irrepressible Churchill*.

94. Quoted in Bocca, *The Adventurous Life of Winston Churchill*.

95. Geoffrey Shakespeare, quoted in Gilbert, *Churchill: A Life*.

96. Quoted in James, *Churchill: A Study in Failure*.

97. Quoted in Manchester, *Visions of Glory.*

98. Quoted in Bocca, *The Adventurous Life of Winston Churchill.*

99. Quoted in James, *Churchill: A Study in Failure.*

100. Quoted in Bocca, *The Adventurous Life of Winston Churchill.*

101. Quoted in James, *Churchill: A Study in Failure.*

102. Quoted in Reader's Digest, *Man of the Century: A Churchill Cavalcade.* Boston: Little, Brown, 1965.

Chapter 6: The Wilderness

103. Quoted in James, *Churchill: A Study in Failure.*

104. Quoted in Manchester, *Alone.*

105. Quoted in Manchester, *Alone.*

106. Quoted in Manchester, *Alone.*

107. Quoted in Halle, *Irrepressible Churchill.*

108. Quoted in Halle, *Irrepressible Churchill.*

109. Quoted in Manchester, *Alone.*

110. Quoted in Gilbert, *Churchill: A Life.*

111. Quoted in James, *Churchill: A Study in Failure.*

112. Quoted in Manchester, *Alone.*

113. Quoted in Manchester, *Alone.*

114. Quoted in Manchester, *Alone.*

115. Quoted in James, *Churchill: A Study in Failure.*

116. Quoted in James, *Churchill: A Study in Failure.*

117. Harold Nicholson, quoted in James, *Churchill: A Study in Failure.*

118. Quoted in Manchester, *Alone.*

119. Quoted in Manchester, *Alone.*

120. Quoted in Manchester, *Alone.*

121. Colin Coote, quoted in Manchester, *Alone.*

122. Quoted in Gilbert, *Churchill: A Life.*

123. Quoted in Gilbert, *Churchill: A Life.*

124. Quoted in Reader's Digest, *Man of the Century.*

Chapter 7: His Finest Hour

125. Quoted in Reader's Digest, *Man of the Century.*

126. Quoted in Gilbert, *Churchill: A Life.*

127. Quoted in Manchester, *Alone.*

128. Quoted in Manchester, *Alone.*

129. Quoted in Gilbert, *Churchill: A Life.*

130. Quoted in Taylor, et al., *Churchill Revised.*

131. Quoted in Manchester, *Alone.*

132. Quoted in Gilbert, *Churchill: A Life.*

133. Quoted in Albjerg, *Winston Churchill.*

134. Quoted in Gilbert, *Churchill: A Life.*

135. Winston S. Churchill, *Their Finest Hour.* Boston: Houghton Mifflin, 1949.

136. Quoted in Reader's Digest, *Man of the Century.*

137. Churchill, *Their Finest Hour.*

138. Quoted in Taylor, et al., *Churchill Revised.*

139. Quoted in Taylor, et al., *Churchill Revised.*

140. Quoted in Bocca, *The Adventurous Life of Winston Churchill.*

141. Quoted in Gilbert, *Churchill: A Life.*

142. Quoted in Wheeler-Bennett, *Action This Day.*

143. Quoted in Gilbert, *Churchill: A Life.*

144. Quoted in Albjerg, *Winston Churchill.*

Chapter 8: Victory and Defeat

145. Quoted in Gilbert, *Churchill: A Life.*

146. Quoted in Gilbert, *Churchill: A Life.*

147. Quoted in Reader's Digest, *Man of the Century.*

148. Quoted in Gilbert, *Churchill: A Life.*

149. Admiral Ernest King, quoted in Albjerg, *Winston Churchill.*

150. Quoted in Albjerg, *Winston Churchill.*

151. Quoted in Wilson (Lord Moran), *Churchill: Taken from the Diaries of Lord Moran.*

152. Quoted in Reader's Digest, *Man of the Century.*

153. Quoted in Gilbert, *Churchill: A Life.*

154. Quoted in Gilbert, *Churchill: A Life*.

155. Quoted in Taylor, et al., *Churchill Revised*.

156. Quoted in Reader's Digest, *Man of the Century*.

157. Quoted in Alan Moorehead, *Churchill and His World*. London: Thames and Hudson, 1960.

158. Quoted in Wheeler-Bennett, *Action This Day*.

159. Quoted in Gilbert, *Churchill: A Life*.

160. General Alan Brooke, quoted in Reader's Digest, *Man of the Century*.

161. Quoted in Reader's Digest, *Man of the Century*.

162. Quoted in Reader's Digest, *Man of the Century*.

163. Quoted in Reader's Digest, *Man of the Century*.

164. Quoted in Gilbert, *Churchill: A Life*.

165. Quoted in Gilbert, *Churchill: A Life*.

166. Quoted in Gilbert, *Churchill: A Life*.

167. Quoted in Albjerg, *Winston Churchill*.

168. Quoted in Gilbert, *Churchill: A Life*.

169. Quoted in Halle, *Irrepressible Churchill*.

Chapter 9: Elder Statesman

170. Quoted in Wilson (Lord Moran), *Churchill: Taken from the Diaries of Lord Moran*.

171. Quoted in Gilbert, *Churchill: A Life*.

172. Quoted in Gilbert, *Churchill: A Life*.

173. Quoted in Gilbert, *Churchill: A Life*.

174. Quoted in Moorehead, *Churchill and His World*.

175. Quoted in Gilbert, *Churchill: A Life*.

176. Rowse, *The Churchills*.

177. Quoted in Gilbert, *Churchill: A Life*.

178. Quoted in Gilbert, *Churchill: A Life*.

179. Quoted in Gilbert, *Churchill: A Life*.

180. Quoted in Gilbert, *Churchill: A Life*.

181. Quoted in Gilbert, *Churchill: A Life*.

182. Quoted in Gilbert, *Churchill: A Life*.

183. Quoted in Gilbert, *Churchill: A Life*.

184. Quoted in Gilbert, *Churchill: A Life*.

185. Quoted in Gilbert, *Churchill: A Life*.

186. Wilson (Lord Moran), *Churchill: Taken from the Diaries of Lord Moran*.

187. Quoted in Gilbert, *Churchill: A Life*.

188. Quoted in Moorehead, *Churchill and His World*.

189. Quoted in Moorehead, *Churchill and His World*.

190. Quoted in Reader's Digest, *Man of the Century*.

191. Quoted in Reader's Digest, *Man of the Century*.

192. Quoted in Moorehead, *Churchill and His World*.

Epilogue: Man of the Century

193. Quoted in Reader's Digest, *Man of the Century*.

194. Taylor, et al., *Churchill Revised*.

195. Hugh Dalton, quoted in Gilbert, *Churchill: A Life*.

196. Rowse, *The Churchills*.

197. Quoted in Gilbert, *Churchill: A Life*.

198. Quoted in Gilbert, *Churchill: A Life*.

For Further Reading

Bruce Bliven Jr., *From Casablanca to Berlin*. New York: Random House, 1965. Simply written, easy-to-read account of World War II in Europe from the Allied landings in North Africa to the surrender of Germany. Relatively few photographs.

Arthur Harold Booth, *The True Story of Sir Winston Churchill*. Chicago: Childrens Press, 1964. Large type and easy-to-read style with ample use of short quotations. Also liberal use of illustrations.

Olivia Coolidge, *Winston Churchill and the Story of Two World Wars*. Boston: Houghton Mifflin, 1960. Despite the title, this is a complete biography, although the sections on the world wars take up the most space (130 pages alone for World War II). Good maps showing the various theaters of war.

Edward F. Dolan, *Portrait in Tyranny*. New York: Dodd, Mead, 1981. Moderately difficult biography of the leader of Nazi Germany. Text is well organized, but the clumping of all the photographs in a central section is awkward.

J.E. Driemen, *Winston Churchill: An Unbreakable Spirit*. Minneapolis: Dillon, 1990. Well-written, moderately difficult biography of Churchill. Contains several pictures not generally seen in other versions.

Trevor Nevitt Dupuy, *European Land Battles, 1944-1945*. New York: Franklin Watts, 1962. Description of the later land war in Europe, starting with the invasion of Normandy in 1944 and continuing through the surrender of Germany. Interesting discussions of the Soviet Union's tactics designed to gain political control in Eastern Europe and of an assassination attempt on Hitler.

——, *Land Battles: North Africa, Sicily, and Italy*. New York: Franklin Watts, 1962. The land battles of World War II from the British reinforcement of North Africa in 1940 to the invasion of Italy. Good description of the North African campaign, including the battles of El Alamein and Tobruk, and the exploits of Rommel and Montgomery, the German and British commanders. Excellent use of maps.

Brendan John Elliott, *Hitler and Germany*. New York: McGraw-Hill, 1968. Excellent account of Hitler's rise and fall. Especially valuable in that it gives the background factors in Germany that made it possible for Nazism to succeed.

Alan Ferrell, *Sir Winston Churchill*. New York: Putnam, 1964. Very animated biography of Churchill up to 1960. Glossary of terms is very helpful, but there are few pictures compared to other versions.

Russell Freedman, *Franklin Delano Roosevelt*. New York: Clarion Books, 1990. Less on World War II than in other biographies, but good account of Roosevelt's career as a politician and his domestic policies. Excellent selection of pictures and cartoons.

Al Hine, *D-Day: The Invasion of Europe*. New York: American Heritage, 1962. Marvelously detailed account of the planning and execution of the invasion of Normandy by the Allies in 1944. Good blend of black-and-white pictures and color illustrations. Could have included more background on question of "second front" during the war.

Dorothy Hoobler and Thomas Hoobler, *The Trenches: Fighting on the Western Front in World War I*. New York: Putnam, 1978. Thorough and factual, and yet a very dramatic presentation showing the horror and futility of war. Gripping photographs of life and death in the trenches. Just as effective are excerpts from diaries and letters.

Mollie Keller, *Winston Churchill*. New York: Franklin Watts, 1984. One in the *Impact Biography Series*. Biography of Churchill written on a junior–senior high level. Not enough pictures to go with length of text.

Robert Matthews, *Winston Churchill*. New York: Bookwright Press, 1989. Short, easy-to-read version of Churchill's life. Amply illustrated with combination of photographs (some in color) and drawings.

Alice Osinski, *Franklin D. Roosevelt*. Chicago: Childrens Press, 1987. Part of the *Encyclopedia of Presidents Series*. Good account of the political factors facing Roosevelt concerning the U.S. entry into World War II as well as the war years.

Quentin James Reynolds, *The Battle of Britain*. New York: Random House, 1953. Good story for younger (elementary grades) readers about the battle between the Royal Air Force and Hitler's *Luftwaffe*. Sparsely illustrated.

———, *Winston Churchill*. New York: Random House, 1963. Biography covers Churchill up to his retirement as prime minister. Brightly written by someone who obviously enjoyed his subject. Very nice feature is the last chapter, an account of the author's meeting with Churchill.

Kenneth G. Richards, *Sir Winston Churchill*. Chicago: Childrens Press, 1968. Part of the *People of Destiny Series*. Type is a little small despite large-book format. Excellent full-page pictures plus several illustrations.

Joshua Rubenstein, *Adolf Hitler*. New York: Franklin Watts, 1984. One of the *Impact Biography Series*. Biographical account of the rise and fall of the Nazi leader. Good, moderately difficult text; short on photographs.

Louis Leo Snyder, *World War I*. New York: Franklin Watts, 1981. Written in good, understandable language. Nicely organized with frequent subheadings to keep the reader oriented.

Conrad R. Stein, *Dunkirk*. Chicago: Childrens Press, 1982. Exciting, dramatic account of the rescue of more than 300,000 English and French troops from almost certain capture by the Germans.

Harold Cecil Vaughn, *The Versailles Treaty*. New York: Franklin Watts, 1975. Designed for the serious, more advanced student, but a very thorough account of the treaty that ended World War I and its consequences, both immediate and long-term.

Works Consulted

Victor L. Albjerg, *Winston Churchill*. New York: Twayne, 1973. Volume 22 of the *Twayne's Rulers and Statesmen of the World Series*. Short yet well-researched and well-documented biography. No photographs, but the frequent use of statistical charts is helpful.

Geoffrey Bocca, *The Adventurous Life of Winston Churchill*. New York: Julian Messner, 1958. Very readable, almost chatty biography with plenty of photographs and cartoons. Lots of good information, despite a few glaring inaccuracies.

Violet Bonham Carter, *Winston Churchill: An Intimate Portrait*. New York: Harcourt, Brace & World, 1965. The author, a lifelong friend of Churchill, was the daughter of a prime minister, Herbert Asquith. Valuable not only for an account of Churchill's early political career, but also for a look at the chief issues of British politics from 1900 through World War I.

Randolph S. Churchill, *Winston S. Churchill, Vol. I, Youth, 1874-1900*. Boston: Houghton Mifflin, 1966. This first volume of the biography written by Churchill's son depends mainly on letters to, from, and about Churchill.

Winston S. Churchill, *Closing the Ring*. Boston: Houghton Mifflin, 1951. This book, the fifth in Churchill's six-volume series on World War II, describes the final victory in North Africa, the Teheran conference, and the invasion of France.

———, *The Gathering Storm*. Boston: Houghton Mifflin, 1948. The first volume in Churchill's account of World War II; gives the background of the war, starting with the end of World War I, and continues until the time Churchill became prime minister.

———, *The Grand Alliance*. Boston: Houghton Mifflin, 1950. The third volume in Churchill's history of World War II tells of the forging of alliances with the United States and the Soviet Union and the victories of 1942.

———, *The Hinge of Fate*. Boston: Houghton Mifflin, 1950. The fourth volume in Churchill's series on World War II describes the strategies and fateful conferences of 1943.

———, *My Early Life*. New York: Scribner's/ Macmillan, 1987. Originally published in 1930 under the title *A Roving Commission*, this is Churchill's account of his first thirty years. Charming, witty, and very self-revealing.

———, *Their Finest Hour*. Boston: Houghton Mifflin, 1949. The second volume in Churchill's account of World War II covers the year 1940 from the fall of France, through the Battle of Britain, to the first victories in North Africa.

———, *Triumph and Tragedy*. Boston: Houghton Mifflin, 1954. The last volume in Churchill's World War II series describes the final victory over Germany and Japan. Ends on a somber note as Churchill discusses the treachery of Stalin and the menace of the Soviet Union.

————, *The World Crisis*. New York: Scribner's, 1923, 1927, 1929, 1931. Churchill's six-volume history of World War I, published over several years. Sometimes self-serving as Churchill tries to defend his own actions and opinions.

Martin Gilbert, *Churchill: A Life*. New York: Henry Holt, 1992. Even at more than a thousand pages, this is but a condensation of the "official," eight-volume biography by Gilbert and Randolph Churchill. A good compromise between the shorter biographies and the exhaustive official version.

Kay Halle, *Irrepressible Churchill*. Cleveland, OH: World, 1966. A thorough collection of the humorous quotes, quips, and retorts that helped make Churchill both famous and feared as a speaker.

Robert Rhodes James, *Churchill: A Study in Failure*. New York: World, 1970. Emphasizes Churchill's mistakes and shortcomings from 1900 to 1939 while only grudgingly acknowledging his successes. A good balance to the biographies that do little except praise.

William Manchester, *Alone: 1932-1940*. New York: Dell, 1988. Second volume (and the last published as of 1993) in Manchester's multivolume biography, *The Last Lion: Winston Spencer Churchill*. Deals with the "wilderness" years. Manchester's books are by far the most entertaining of the Churchill biographies consulted.

————, *Visions of Glory: 1874-1932*. New York: Dell, 1983. First volume in *The Last Lion: Winston Spencer Churchill*. Wonderfully readable account of Churchill's early life. Manchester is especially good at setting the stage by describing the state of Britain and the British Empire.

Ralph G. Martin, *Jennie, the Life of Lady Randolph Churchill: The Romantic Years, 1854-1895*. Englewood Cliffs, NJ: Prentice Hall, 1969. First of two-part biography of Churchill's American mother. Less critical toward her treatment of her elder son than are other accounts.

Alan Moorehead, *Churchill and His World*. London: Thames and Hudson, 1960. Good general biography with an excellent selection of photographs. The postscript by Douglas Sutherland, on Churchill's death and funeral, is especially moving.

Reader's Digest, *Man of the Century: A Churchill Cavalcade*. Boston: Little, Brown, 1965. This biography was pieced together from more than fifty original sources. The editorial technique makes for choppy reading, but the work provides a wealth of Churchill anecdotes.

A.L. Rowse, *The Churchills: The Story of a Family*. New York: Harper & Row, 1966. A combination and abridgement of Rowse's two earlier books, *The Early Churchills* and *The Churchills*. Traces the family from the 1600s through the various dukes of Marlborough to Winston Churchill.

A.J.P. Taylor, Robert Rhodes James, J.H. Plumb, Basil Liddell Hart, and Anthony Storr, *Churchill Revised*. New York: Dial Press, 1969. Four essays pointing up Churchill's mistakes and shortcomings as, respectively, a statesman, a politician, a historian, and a military strategist, plus a concluding psychological profile.

John Wheeler-Bennett, ed., *Action This Day*. London: St. Martin's Press, 1969. First-person accounts of what it was like to work with Churchill on a day-to-day basis during and after World War II. Written by seven members of Churchill's staff in part to refute some of the statements in the book by Lord Moran, Churchill's doctor.

Charles Wilson (Lord Moran), *Churchill: Taken from the Diaries of Lord Moran*. Boston: Houghton Mifflin, 1966. Excerpts from the diaries of Churchill's personal physician give good insights into Churchill's personality and fascinating behind-the-scenes looks at the Teheran and Yalta conferences.

Index

Credits

Cover photo by Archive Photos

AP/Wide World Photos, 10, 12, 16, 20, 29, 69, 73 (both), 74, 94, 100, 110, 112

Archive Photos, 41, 63, 64, 95 (bottom), 102, 105, 106, 111

Archive Photos/Express Newspapers, 14, 24

Archive Photos/Hirz, 49

The Bettmann Archive, 15, 26, 28, 31, 34, 36 (both), 39, 42, 43, 47 (both), 51, 52, 57, 72

Library of Congress, 68, 99

National Archives, 30, 50, 54, 78 (left), 80, 82, 84, 85, 87, 89, 90 (both), 93, 95 (top), 96, 98, 113

UPI/Bettmann, 11, 46, 55, 62, 66, 67, 76, 78 (right), 79, 86, 103

About the Author

William W. Lace is a native of Fort Worth, Texas. He holds a bachelor's degree from Texas Christian University, a master's from East Texas State University, and a doctorate from the University of North Texas. After working for newspapers in Baytown, Texas, and Fort Worth, he joined the University of Texas at Arlington as sports information director and later became the director of the news service. He is now vice chancellor for public affairs at Tarrant County Junior College in Fort Worth. He and his wife, Laura, live in Arlington and have two children. Lace's other books include biographies of baseball player Nolan Ryan and artist Michelangelo, a history of the Hundred Years' War, and a history of Elizabethan England.